D1176495

Ex
Libris

The taste
of
new wine

by KEITH MILLER

Habitation of
dragons

GUIDEPOSTS ASSOCIATES, INC.

Carmel, New York

INTRODUCTION

In this two-in-one book selection, Guideposts is greatly pleased to bring to our readers Keith Miller, an exciting new voice in the field of Christian writing. He offers solutions to our contemporary personal problems that are both challenging and sensible.

There is nothing esoteric about Keith Miller's thinking. He is a layman who, though theologically trained, speaks like a layman. When he discusses problems relating to marriage, children, the church, jobs, friendships, politics, he speaks to them with the understanding and sensitivity of a man who has had first hand dealings with all of them.

"The Taste of New Wine" is one of the biggest religious best sellers because it bares the soul of a good man struggling to do God's will in the face of all the familiar temptations to go along with the crowd. It is a rare personal adventure of modern man's aspiration to lead a Christian life every hour of the day.

"Habitation of Dragons" is Keith Miller's latest and most practical book of spiritual guidance. As many as 42 different everyday problems are treated. The method is unique, each problem receiving a very effective 4-step process: prayer, Scriptural reference, a highlight from literature, and a personal experience.

Here is a particularly interesting day-at-a-time devotional exercise. From this abundance of 42 subjects treated with deep spiritual sensitivity, any reader should find new paths through the dragon-infested jungle of modern life.

In whatever order you choose to read, we think you will be inspired and rewarded. Keith Miller has mined this material from personal experience and study; now it's up to you to assay its value and apply it in the search for God's real meaning for your life.

The Editors

The taste
of
new wine

by KEITH MILLER

GUIDEPOSTS ASSOCIATES, INC.

Carmel, New York

FOREWORD

In June, 1961, when I went to Laity Lodge for the initial retreat, I little knew the wealth of human dividends that were in store for me. The finest of these unexpected dividends was the friendship of Keith Miller whom I then met for the first time. From the beginning it was evident that in this man was the combination of intellectual sharpness and spiritual depth which our time so sorely needs. Subsequent encounters, during the past four years, both at Earlham College and elsewhere, have verified the original judgment and increased the original hope. And now, that the book has been written, I am glad to help to introduce it to potential readers in this country and abroad.

The book *The Taste of New Wine* is not a book about religion, but rather a work which belongs to the category of witness. Keith Miller does not, primarily, discuss witness; he provides, instead, a first-hand testimony of what has transpired in his own life thus far. The book is an interim report concerning the way in which God has reached him in both pain and joy.

It is no accident that the book makes abundant use of the pronoun "I." There are people who seek, self-consciously, to avoid the employment of this pronoun, but Keith Miller has been wise not to engage in such a futile effort. After all, the most important thing a man has to

5

say is not some speculation about what may be true, but rather a direct and unself-conscious reporting of what has occurred in first-hand experience. The only testimony which has any value is that which necessitates the first person. It is not possible to find anything more basic than the report of one who says, simply and humbly, "Whereas I was blind, now I see."

There is only one pronoun nobler than "I," and that is "Thou." The author of this book seeks to order his life in direct response to One who is best understood as the Eternal Thou. In short, his religion is centered in prayer and he knows that a man has made a beginning in prayer when, abandoning mere discussion, he sincerely says, "O God, You." When so many are vague on this point, or even impersonal in their emphasis, the words of our author come to us with a refreshing straightforwardness.

Keith Miller's book will, I predict, have a wide and appreciative reading for many reasons, but chiefly because his mood is wholly unapologetic. He takes a stand and he is clear enough to let the reader know what the stand is. There is no person whom I know whose book I should rather recommend than this one.

D. ELTON TRUEBLOOD

PREFACE

For the past three years I have directed and participated in various conferences at an interdenominational lay center in Southwest Texas called Laity Lodge. I have sensed an exciting new movement of renewal in the lives of Christians from all over America; but I have been increasingly concerned about one recurring type of question asked each week by laymen and women. Most of these people are officers in local Christian congregations; and many have been denominational leaders for years. Yet again and again, when we ask them during a conference to write personal, anonymous questions, they secretly tell us that they do not know how to pray, how to witness to other people about Christ without being embarrassed, how to simply communicate with their wives and families, or how to approach their vocational and social lives as committed Christians.

This book is written to these people. It is a distillation of nine years of struggling alone and with small groups to find a way to live and communicate as a layman the amazing power and love inherent in the Christian Gospel. There are many ways to discuss the doctrines of Christianity; but when it comes to living the Christian life, I have come to believe that each man has only one story to tell. And recorded here is mine.

ACKNOWLEDGMENTS

It is impossible to acknowledge specifically the help of those people whose lives, writings and counsel over these past years may appear in this book as insights apparently "discovered" by me. I have tried, where practical, to give credit to the original human donor. But I am afraid many of the ideas have been so mingled and integrated that they have become a part of my own spiritual bloodstream. I can only say "thank you" to those of you who may see your influence in print here.

Since I have spoken so often on the same programs with Howard Butt, Jr. these past three years and studied so recently with Dr. D. Elton Trueblood, I have probably stolen most freely, though unconsciously, from them. The errors and inadequacies which appear, however, are my own. I would never have written this book if it had not been for the encouragement of my teacher and friend, Elton Trueblood, to whom I owe so much—not only for his guidance in my life but for his immediate help and suggestions in reading this manuscript.

I would like to thank Mrs. Howard E. Butt, Sr. and Howard and Barbara Dan Butt for encouraging me to do this writing while working as director at Laity Lodge. Also I want to express deep gratitude to Mr. and Mrs. Carl Newton and to Gene Warr who, through their generosity, helped make it possible for us to study at the Earlham School of Religion. Mrs. Bill Lee, who typed the early sketches of this manuscript, gave not only mechanical help but the invaluable support of enthusiasm. I am also indebted to our friend, Gladys Ranger, for her assistance in typing the final copies.

To the editors of the "Review and Expositor" I am grateful for permission to use part of the material appearing here in chapters one and seven which appeared earlier in that journal. Similiarly, I want to thank the editors of "Faith at Work" with regard to material found in chapters three and six. Also, grateful acknowledgement is hereby made to the authors and publishers set out in the footnotes and to Mrs. William Temple for permission to quote from the works mentioned in the following pages.

Finally, I owe most of all from a human perspective to my wife, Mary Allen, whose loyalty and calm confidence from the beginning that I would complete this manuscript and that it would be published shattered me into getting it finished. She has listened to and loved me through it all. It is to her that this book is dedicated.

KEITH MILLER
Laity Lodge
Leakey, Texas

CONTENTS

Chapter 1

"Something is loosed to change the stricken world."

STEPHEN VINCENT BENET

OUT OF THE FERMENT

About five years ago I stumbled onto a new style of life which is flooding into the main stream of the church today. This new life can be seen in the experience and witness of thousands of business and professional men and women and Christian ministers and their families in America today. These people, clergy and laymen, have in many different ways realized some striking facts. For years the New Testament's call for total commitment of the whole man—with his vocation, family and avocations—had been seemingly lost, drowned in the midst of the noises of building a better America, a better world, and ironically a better "Church." Thousands of yards of concrete were poured into hundreds of new sanctuaries, parish halls and parking lots. Millions of new people were recruited to membership in church activity. Yet somehow in the process something of the wholeness of Christ slipped through our fingers. An obvious separation was allowed to grow between denominations and an even worse separation between a living faith in any denomination and one's secular vocation.

On Main Street the wind of the Spirit grew still, and it is difficult to see where it "listeth" as the concrete of our generation's progress has hardened. In the business and professional worlds' eyes Christ has been relegated at best to a position of Lord of the specifically "religious" activities. And as an active and dedicated churchman I had seen from the inside that to call the Christ of the New Testament *Lord* of the average congregation's *contemporary activity* in any true sense was preposterous.

Contemporaneously with the recognition of these facts there were

indications in dozens of different geographical and ecclesiastical areas
of the stirring of a new order of Christians, an order which has transcended denominational and vocational lines and the members of which
travel hundreds of thousands of miles a year to encourage each other,
to have a living Christian fellowship, and to struggle together with
stark and actual problems they face in common. These men and
women are a serious yet amazingly happy band of converted Christian
lay people in America. They are alert. Many of them are unusually
successful in their secular vocational pursuits. Most are active in their
own denomination's witness. Yet there is nothing of the spiritual grayness of the institution about them. They are *alive* in a striking way!

There is no organization; there are no dues, no memberships—in
fact there is only one reason they can be called a "band." They have
in common only the Lordship of Jesus Christ and a deep conviction
that His call is to the *whole man*—vocation and all. When investigated,
the only credentials this group can present to their sometimes skeptical
denominations are the hundreds of transformed and growing lives in
the wake of their witness.[1] They are often disturbing. For these modern
disciples are not satisfied with abstract statements of doctrine—however accurate. They feel a strange dichotomy between the church's
doctrinal statements and the problems of the market place as they
actually are.

Out of the resulting frustration has come a feeling that the church
is too "philosophical" in its orientation and that the philosophic mind
easily forgets its base in the actualities of a man's life. It can get lost
in abstractions. Soren Kierkegaard said of Hegel that when he asked
the philosopher in effect for directions to a street address in Copen-
hagen he was given only a map of Europe.

A map of Europe or any other continent will not do for this pilgrimage. This new order of "live ones" has realized that the universality of Christ's message is only intelligible as it is focused in *specific*
lives and *specific* vocational situations which demand specific decisions

1. "The ultimate verification of our religion consists of the changed lives to
which it can point and for which it is responsible." (See D. Elton Trueblood,
Foundations for Reconstruction, New York: Harper and Brothers, 1961, p.
107.)

for or against Christ's will as it can be perceived in the struggles for power, for prestige, and for material goods.

This new fellowship was brought into existence when some deeply concerned laymen found the institutional church defensive concerning the structured programs and in many cases unprepared to face the problems confronting this new body of missionaries—to the specialized vocational life of our generation. Some Baptist, Methodist, Episcopal, and Presbyterian laymen who were trying to commit *their whole* lives to Christ found that they had more in common with each other than with some of the pillars of their own denominations.

These men and women were not the "Junior-Preachers" of a day gone by. They were not like clerical assistants wanting only more academic knowledge than their fellows about the theology and worship of the church—though they want this too—; instead they constitute a new body of disciples concerned about the *love* of God and saying instinctively and from their own experience that, "the knowledge of God is very far from the love of Him."[2]

Although many of these business men, attorneys, physicians and politicians are not academically sophisticated in their theological training, they are turning to the Living Christ as their Teacher and to the Bible as a valid revelation of the nature of God and man. Consequently, although they realize the deep need for further knowledge, their lives and their message are close to the heart of the Christian Way as perceived by remarkable Christians of all ages: "The heart of religion is not an opinion about God such as philosophy might reach as a conclusion of its arguments; it is a personal relationship with God."[3] "Faith is not the holding of correct doctrines but personal fellowship with the Living God . . . *What is offered to man's apprehension in any specific Revelation is not truth concerning God but the Living God Himself.*"[4]

In their examination of the Scriptures as converted Christians, men and women are discovering that institutional churchmanship, as it is commonly known in the United States, simply does not express for

---

2. Blaise Pascal, *Pascal's Pensees*, E. P. Dutton and Co., Inc., 1958, p. 79.
3. William Temple, *Nature, Man and God*, London: Macmillan Co. Ltd., 1956, p. 54.
4. Ibid., p. 322 (Archbishop Temple's italics).

them the wholeness of the new life they are experiencing. Christ is tearing out the partitions in men's souls between vocation, church, and home and making a one room dwelling place for Himself in their whole lives. People are re-discovering that "religion is not a form of experience existing separately from other forms of experience. It is the transfiguration of the whole of experience."[5]

To those of us who are part of this new going forth, there is an excitement akin to that reflected in the Book of Acts. But after the first burst of enthusiasm there have also been questions, serious questions, from church leaders and from those people who are newly involved, both ministers and laymen, in this evangelical renewal.

What is it about this "new life" which makes its bearers no longer satisfied merely to sit in the pews and on committees or even to stand in pulpits? Why are the old wineskins feeling a disturbing tenseness as the new wine is fermenting? What is this new style of life? What makes the difference?

---

5. J. H. Oldham, *Life is Commitment*, New York: Association Press, 1959, p. 96.

Chapter 2

"*The heart is deceitful above all things, and desperately corrupt; who can understand it?*"

(Jeremiah 17:9 RSV)

A NEW KIND OF HONESTY

During my first four years as an active adult churchman I had taught two Sunday School classes, served on numerous committees and on the vestries of two churches. These were fine churches, filled with good, substantial people. But one of the constant sources of frustration was that in Sunday School classes, teachers meetings, committee meetings, and even vestry meetings in the church there was an amazing lack of basic honesty. It wasn't so much that people lied. We just had an unspoken agreement not to press the truth—when it seemed that the truth might hurt the leaders or someone else's feelings—or really rock the boat. We evidently felt that being honest in such cases would be cruel or tactless. Consequently we lived in a world of subtle duplicity of which we Christians were the contributing cause.

You may say that this does not apply to your church; but I have talked to so many laymen and leaders in the various denominations about this that I am convinced it is almost universally true.

Although I had always tried desperately to be honest and to have integrity, even in the meetings I mentioned, I have only recently realized that *true* honesty has a very deceptive and elusive quality . . . *especially* among those of us who call ourselves Christians. Our tremendous drive for social acceptance and toward conformity in our time is causing us to train our children to be a generation of young liars who do not even realize they are lying. As so many thinking people have pointed out recently, the current and growing moral decay in this country is not so much to be attributed to the under-

21

privileged parent in the slums as to *us*, the middle and upper class American churchmen . . . laymen and ministers.

We train our children to be subtly dishonest almost from the crib. In my mind's eye I can still see a little four or five year old girl sitting in the aisle of a crowded department store several years ago. She was howling with great feeling as her mother was trying to drag her to her feet. She had evidently sat down to play in the dust while her mother was looking at something on the counter. A large man had walked by in the crowded aisle and stepped on the child's hand. Being human, she screamed at the top of her lungs. Everyone looked. What was the mother's reaction? She jerked the little girl up from the floor in embarrassment and said in her ear, "Shh . . ., don't cry in front of all these people." I still remember the confused look on the child's face as she stared at her throbbing, swollen hand.

Or, when a little girl is twelve and gets ready to go to a gala party, what does the mother say? Does she advise her daughter to "Have a good time. Try to look for people who aren't happy and help them to have a nice time too?"

No, she more likely says, "Now listen honey, if they are not friendly with you, keep smiling. Don't let them know you are unhappy"— no, don't let them know that your heart is broken . . . keep smiling.

So on and on we train our children to *look* happy and successful, to hide their true feelings, their true needs. By the time they are grown, their natural reaction is to put forth immediately the image expected of them in almost any given situation—regardless of how they may honestly feel about that situation.

The result is our churches are filled with people who outwardly look contented and at peace but inwardly are crying out for someone to love them . . . just as they are—confused, frustrated, often frightened, guilty, and often unable to communicate even within their own families. But the *other* people in the church *look* so happy and contented that one seldom has the courage to admit his own deep needs before such a self-sufficient group as the average church meeting appears to be.

What am I suggesting?—that we suddenly drop our masks and reveal ourselves naked to each other and the church with all our secret greed and lust and hate and resentments? No, but I am suggesting that we must realize that our fellowship is incurably crippled until and unless we recognize and face squarely the nature and extent of our deceitfulness with God, with each other, and with ourselves.

I am convinced that although honesty may not be the front doorway to the kingdom of God, it is the *latchstring* to every doorway in His house. And yet, I have found honesty with one's self to be the most elusive state in my own Christian life. Thinking Christians have always been baffled by their own deceitful behavior. In the seventh chapter of Romans, Paul gives us his classic statement of this experience: "I do not understand my own actions. For I do not do what I want, but I do the very thing I hate." (Romans 7:15 RSV.)

The late Archbishop William Temple came very close to the truth, I believe, when he indicated the nature of our deceiving of ourselves. He realized that our *true willing* is what controls our acts. The reason we are disappointed in our actions is because though we consciously wish to be good we really *will* our own self satisfaction. And until our true willing (which is mostly unconscious) is redirected, we are trapped and don't know why.[1] At this point in his own struggling to try to understand the unreliability of his behavior, Paul cries out, "Wretched man that I am! Who will deliver me from this body of death?" (Romans 7:24 RSV). Who can let me see who I really am . . . what I in fact really want beneath my valiant words? It seems clear to me now, after years of self deception as a converted Christian, that the first thing we need to know if we are truly to become new disciples and apostles of our Lord is that through years of habit and reaction to our social melee we are deeply, though unconsciously, deceptive with ourselves.

To see how this is so, look in any of your areas of temptation (e.g. that one which disturbs you most continually). Of course, if you say you have no temptation, no sin, the New Testament is pretty clear in its witness to the fact that you have already deceived yourself and are void of the truth (I John 1:8-10). In any case, those of us who have been conscious of temptation, how does it work? What process

---

1. William Temple, *Op. Cit.*, See excellent discussion of this point in Lecture IX, Freedom and Determinism," p. 223f.

does one go through in facing an attractive temptation? My own experience has too often been that I say to myself silently, "I don't want to do this thing. I do not want to resent this person, be jealous of that person, or lust for that woman. I do not want to be this kind of a man. I do not want to! Do not want to." . . . and then I succumb and resent them, gossip about them, or lust for them before I know it. Afterwards I say to God, "I don't know what is the matter with me. I don't *want* to be this way."

But this process and conclusion illustrate the self deception which tears the rug out from under our relationship with Christ and each other and leaves us disillusioned and bewildered. For I believe the truth of the matter is that at the motivating center of our lives we *really will* to do those things which we do in our weakness. Unconsciously or consciously I deeply want to destroy you with gossip if you have hurt me acutely. I really want to lust for you if you attract me in this way. And *until I see this* I am bewildered by my seeming failure to do what the real me wants to do. I have become convinced that the *real* me is not *failing* but *succeeding* when I succumb to temptation. Because the nature of the real me is to will to gratify my deep egocentric desires.

I (unconsciously) want subtly to control people in a business situation, so I strike back when you threaten to destroy my reputation, my power to control in a committee meeting. If I really wanted only Christ's will (as I claim) then when you remind me in front of a nominating committee that I never get things in on time, I should say, "Thank you for calling this to our attention. I see that it affects the possibilities of my doing as good a job as chairman of this committee as old Joe would. And I think he might do a better job." But this is *not* my reaction. My reaction is one of anger and resentment. I am furious that you have brought to light before this group one of my cardinal weaknesses. And I submit that we all react this way in certain areas because our real desire is to satisfy our own self-centered needs.

I do not know this because it has been *consciously* true. Because it has not (for the most part). Consciously, as a committed Christian, I have striven to be selfless for Christ. But over these past nine years my day in, day out reactions have proved to me time and time again that I actually want my own way more than God's. For example, what else could account for the secret wave of satisfaction I feel when someone who has been opposed to me is discredited or makes a big mistake so that I look better? If I really wanted Christ's will more than my own fulfillment I would be hurt that this child of His was suffering.

Or in my own family, when my wife puts her finger on some uncouth or selfish little habit of mine—if I really wanted only God's will I would say, "Thank you darling, for pointing out this grievous fault in my character; my goal is to eliminate such things." . . . But this is *not* my normal reaction. All of these reactions and many, many, more have shown me in living color that my primary and unconscious motivation has been to gratify myself.

But if this is true—that we have really deceived ourselves as committed Christians, why have we done this? And more important, what can we do about it? Indeed, "Who can free us from this body of death?"

The first step for me was to realize starkly and without excuse that I *have* been dishonest with myself, consciously and unconsciously— and to ask myself why. William Law has said in essence that if a man imputes a selfish motive to his actions every time he will be correct in an overwhelming number of instances. But why are we so blinded by ourselves? Why can't we just admit that we basically want our own way and that we will go to great lengths to get it? Why do we delude ourselves or pretend that we are such unselfish people?

First, I think we are unreal about ourselves, even as Christians, because we are afraid that if people find out what we are actually like inside, behind the mask, find out that we really don't honestly want to be with them socially as much as we imply, they will not accept us and therefore we won't be able to fulfill our self-centered needs through our associations with them. You think this is too strong an indictment to level at us churchmen? Think it over.

In one's own experience this is very subtle. I believe that many young women join exclusive socio-civic club groups not because of any burning desire to help the helpless, but because (1) it is an honor to be asked. And (2) belonging helps one project an image of benevolence which implies that we are something which we are not—unselfish and deeply concerned about the poor. Of course, there are thousands of exceptions, but the tragedy is that one can even use the term "exception" to describe them.

A more clear-cut example of our dishonesty is our continual tendency to accept social invitations to go places we actually do not want to go to be with people we honestly do not care about being with. When one analyzes *why*, he is drawn to the conclusion that we go for fear we will not be asked back to some more places we do not want to go. And if this rejection took place, we are afraid we might be pushed out of the aura of "their" acceptance which we suspect is the arena of our self-fulfillment.

You may be thinking, "Thank goodness that is not my problem. I am certainly not dependent on the approval of the crowd for my security." And there have been times when I, too, have reacted against this herd living and become independent. At such times I, too, have said, "Thank God I'm not in that trap. I don't care what the crowd thinks." But in retrospect I realize that the opinion of those other "independents" to whom I was addressing my remarks meant a great deal to me. I have a friend who is a fine Christian who states publicly that he doesn't care what people think about him; and yet this man cares more than almost anyone I know about what a *select few* people think. He has merely changed the arena and audience on whom he depends for ego-gratification from "the crowd," to a few discerning Christians—but the problem is the same; and the unconscious dishonesty with one's self even deeper.

In short, I believe that we deceive ourselves about our selfishness and egocentricity because we are afraid a revelation of our true nature would alienate us from our chosen associates. Further, we cannot face the Biblical implication that the true nature of man is such that each of us is really engaged (however unconsciously) in the building of the kingdom of Keith or Joe (or whatever *your* name is). We must find an appropriate audience because a kingdom with no subjects to respect the king is untenable. (And this is true whether one is a man or woman or whether one's audience is a national one or only a single husband or child.) To build up our images, and our kingdoms, we are subtly dishonest about any thoughts or desires or habits we have which do not fit our projected image for fear our sub-jects will discover our secret: that inside, behind the facade, we are not really kingly or queenly at all; but instead, in our intimate actions we are the servants, the slaves, of our resentments, our jealousies, our lusts, and our anxieties and insecurities. The more kingly, the more self-sufficient an image we try to project, the more we must dishonestly deny in a hundred ways that we are self centered little children at heart bent on our own self-gratification.

Although Paul and the other New Testament writers had not heard of Freud's discovery of the unconscious and were therefore not looking for symptoms of its activity among Christians, the very presence and content of the Epistles show clearly that these writers were well aware that the lustful self-centeredness of a man does not automatically end when he consciously becomes a member of the church. We in the modern Protestant world have somehow intimated that because Christ has overcome man's basic sinful condition, his basic separation, an intelligent intellectual assent by us to that proposition in joining the church is supposed to make us automatically God-centered and not self-centered people.

Consequently our modern church is filled with many people who look pure, sound pure, and are inwardly sick of themselves, their weak-nesses, their frustration, and the lack of reality around them in the church. Our non-Christian friends feel either "that bunch of nice un-troubled people would never understand my problems;" or the more perceptive pagans who know us socially or professionally feel that we Christians are either grossly protected and ignorant about the human situation or are out-and-out hypocrites who will not confess the sins and weakness our pagan friends know intuitively to be universal.

So the new style of life being experienced in the church today be-gins, I believe, with a new kind of honesty—an honesty which really *believes* that *all* of us have sinned and fallen short of the glory of God. We believe that the nature of man is to be so centered in himself that even as committed Christians "we deceive ourselves and the truth is not in us." And by recognizing that all our efforts and enterprises both in and out of the church are tainted to the core with self-centered desires for recognition, power, or social acceptance, we can come to God anew as helpless little children. In honest confession and acceptance of His perception and power we can begin *now* to live together the abundant life of freedom and openness Christ came to bring all who would come to Him in this way.

And we can begin to live this life not in some far off time or condition but in the present moment . . . in the *now*. But we must make a new beginning.

Chapter 3

".. . if anyone is in Christ he is a new creation; the old has passed away, behold, the new has come."

(II Corinthians 5:17 RSV)

A NEW KIND OF BEGINNING

How does one describe a new beginning with God as the motivating center of his life without basing his description on some vague mystical feeling? How does a man who wants to have intellectual integrity describe the experience of encountering God existentially as the personal, the immediate and limitless *Thou* in his life? The attempt to explain this unfolding in a layman's contemporary experience is complicated by the fact that Christ did not leave a reasoned theological explanation. All He seems to have pointed to and promised His followers was a *"way"*— a way across the chasm between God and man, between man and man . . . and between a man and his real nature.

The Gospel of Jesus Christ calls for a different understanding of the nature of truth than most of us have been educated to have. Where the scientific method has been dominant in a Christian layman's education, he sometimes thinks of God as a Master Thinker, or Philosophical Theologian. In a real sense I believe God is presented in the Christian revelation as more of a living and creative artist than a philosopher or theologian. A philosopher in order to be universal presents an argument or dialogue covering every possible contingency; but an artist in attempting to be universal is terribly specific. For example, to describe the universal experience of frustration, or of questioning about life, a poet gives us a picture of one specific mouse in a field, one Grecian urn, one country church yard . . . and in these specific scenes or experiences all men can see frustration, and the basic mystery of their own lives.

Christianity says that when God wanted to convey the truth about

His infinite love for all men He made that love incarnate in a *single* life . . . and in the action of that life all kinds of men have been able to perceive His love's universal extent through the enlightening work of God's Spirit. History has shown again and again that in trying to transmit the essence of the *Life* Christ demonstrated and continues to offer each of us, we cannot speak adequately in propositional terms. We are forced to turn to the language of living experience. In the last analysis we are all reduced to the witness of "that which we have seen and heard" in our own lives.

I do not know any "general rules" for living life as a business man and father and husband consciously committed to the Living Christ. I know of no scholars in this field. All I can do is to witness to insights received on one adventure of faith which continues to change my own life and that of my family. The fact that these insights have been verified in the Scriptures, in the lives of Christians in the Church's History, and in the experience of dozens of contemporary men and women who have come to Laity Lodge has made me believe that they represent more than a subjective pilgrimage. This is the way it began:

By the time I was eighteen years old I was a great success. (At least at the time it seemed that I was.) In a large high school I had won honors in basketball, dramatic reading, class plays, had been elected president of the senior class, and finally king of the school. Life's opportunities appeared to be limitless, in spite of the fact that it was 1945 and we were in the midst of the Second World War.

Three months after graduation, I saw the western world sitting on the brink of an explosion of joy and relief, anticipating momentarily the official word that the war was over. But fifteen days before the war ended we received word that my only brother, whom I idolized, had been killed in a plane crash while serving in the Air Force. That night I remember sitting alone on the back steps in tears.

We had always been a close family, and my mother's reaction was one of deep grief, as was my father's. As I sat there terribly alone, I felt that someday I had to find the meaning of life. I felt that I had to pour myself into it twice as much, since Earle would not get a chance to live it at all. During those next few months my mother got continually worse, and finally had a nervous breakdown a little over a year later.

The strain on my father had been too much also, and at about the same time he had a heart attack. I had left for the Navy two weeks after my brother's death; and after eleven months in the Navy, I had been released to go to college. My parents were sick; and as I began to get to know them as one adult knows others, they poured out their souls separately before me. I realized that although I had been living with them nineteen years, I did not really know these people—nor did they know each other. They did not realize the anguish caused by the little things in their own lives which hurt and frustrated each other; and I felt that neither actually understood about the hopes and dreams in the other's soul . . . and yet we had been a close family and had known much love and happiness. I began to realize that there was a great deal of life which I had not counted on.

I went to college on a basketball scholarship and the G.I. bill. During the Christmas vacation of my sophomore year I was traveling across the state to a fraternity party. We were driving very fast when the right front wheel slipped off onto the highway shoulder which had been washed away. The driver tried to turn the car suddenly back onto the highway, and it went completely out of control. There was a long screech, and I closed my eyes.

Suddenly, I felt like a rock in a tin can as we bounced and rolled 270 yards down a long hillside, over and over, five and a half times. When the car stopped it was on its side and I was on my face against the groundward side. There was dust everywhere. I lay still for a moment and then opened my eyes. There, beside me was a pair of legs, and I thought my friend who had been riding with me in the back seat had been cut in two. But then the legs began to move and I realized he had been thrown face first out of the rear view window and was struggling to pull his legs free.

When he got out and turned around, he smiled. His face seemed to sort of fall apart from the impact. Blood was covering his face.

I tried to get up on my hands and knees but my head fell, and I realized that I had broken my neck. I kept trying to think, "What happens to you when you break your neck?" All I could remember was that you died. Somehow I wanted to get out of that car to die.

It was just about sunset, and the cold grayness of December was closing in around us. I told my friend what had happened, and then asked him if he could help me get out. He was unhurt except for facial cuts. So I held my head with both hands, realizing that I had to keep my spine straight, and he dragged me out of the car. I remember as he was trying to help me, looking around and seeing spectators standing around the car watching, afraid to help for fear of becoming involved. One man was even taking a photograph, and I thought to myself, "What a cold bunch of -------- these are!"

My friend, Bob, put his overcoat on the ground and helped me lie down beside the road, then covered me with my own. I lay there an hour and a half waiting for the ambulance. I remember lying beside the highway and praying very simply. I was very much awake. As I prayed I had a strange feeling of peace that permeated my consciousness. I thought to myself, "What a shame to find out that this kind of peace is a reality so late in life." For the first time I was not afraid to die. I realized at that moment that even in this tragedy which might be the end of life for me there was Something very personal, very real which was more important than anything else I had ever known.

But I got over the broken neck . . . and the feeling of peace.

The next couple of years were filled with turmoil inside, and yet a turmoil mingled with a great deal of joy. For although I was bearing the burdens of the family in trying to keep my parents afloat emotionally and spiritually as their lives were drawing to an end, I also found and fell in love with a girl at school, whose love changed my life. Although I had recovered from the broken neck I had also pushed God back into the corner of my life as I re-entered the stream of competition for grades and attention. Except that by now a lot of that frantic life had lost its savor. Some of the fresh naivete had been replaced by methodical knowledge of how to get things done in the world of people. In my sophomore year I was elected president of my fraternity, and found out that I was on the verge of having ulcers the same month.

Not many months later I remember sitting in a hospital room, beside the bed of my father who was dying. I was praying again and wringing my hands in helpless frustration. His stomach ulcers had perforated, and because of his heart condition they could not operate.

I was sitting beside his bed watching him bleed to death internally. I loved him very much. As I sat there helplessly shaking my head, a small Roman Catholic nun, one of the Sisters at the hospital, came into the room. She walked over to the other side of my father's bed, picked up his hand patted it. She said to him gently, "Can you hear me?"

He said, "Yes," very weakly.

She said to him, "Have you ever accepted Jesus Christ as your Lord and Savior?"

He shook his head, "No."

Then she asked him quietly and matter of factly, "Would you like to do this?"

There was a pause, and then he said, "Oh *yes.*"

She said to him, "Then repeat after me: I accept you, Jesus Christ, as my Lord and Savior."

He did, and then he twisted in the bed and died.

After my father's death I graduated from college and went to work for a major oil company. I had married Mary Allen in my senior year. We were sent to that company's exploration office in Southwest Texas, near the Rio Grande valley. In those next months as I drove through that vast desert land near the Mexican border, I came to love the silence, the stillness, and the vastness very much. I became fascinated by the changes in the desert. The white, hot noonday blast with the heat waves rising continually and visibly off the highway ahead and off the desert to the side would change into an amazing coolness. The magnificent sunsets hinted at something wonderful and very real beyond the horizon. Then suddenly the total blackness of night and coldness would envelope it all. As I drove through that vast desert country alone, day after day, I began to sense something of the majesty and the silent power of God in the world. There awoke in me a realization that I must somehow learn more about God and find out about Jesus Christ—who was supposed to *be* God.

This restlessness grew until one night at home in the middle of the night I woke Mary Allen and said, "Honey, I've got to go back to school to find out about God."

She was sleepy and surprised, but after a moment said, "I'll go with you, but how will we do it?"

We had a new baby and some debts to pay. I said I didn't know but thought maybe we ought to pray about it; and we did. I did not have any desire to become an ordained minister but that seemed to be what the kind of interest I had had, pointed to. This seemingly was what one did when his commitment and interest reached a certain point.

When the men at the oil company office found out that I was going to study theology many of them did not know quite how to react. I was the first person from that particular office to go to Divinity School. They didn't know how to send me off. They had a way which was standard for sending people off to other offices. They didn't know if this would be appropriate. But since there was no precedent for a change, the final social functions engineered by our friends were empowered by the usual spirits, which did not seem at all incongruous at the time.

I remember one of my closest friends at the office putting his arm around my neck and leaning rather heavily on me at about 2:00 o'clock one morning and saying to me through deeply sincere and slightly watery eyes, "Buddy, you'll never make it!" And with this send-off we went to live in the East.

I had enrolled in a graduate theological school, realizing that God, that Reality, must lie in this direction. The Church said that it did and the world thought that it might. Off we went.

But regardless of any preparation we had had, when we got to the school I soon sensed that for me there was something terribly wrong at Divinity School. Some of these young men seemed more full of themselves than had the men at the fraternity to which I belonged. There seemed to be an intellectual competitiveness that was very keen, and somehow unloving. But this I understood, and began to try to compete with the best of them. As the weeks rolled by I felt in my soul that this couldn't be the answer to life, since it was only a religious version of the same kind of competitiveness which I already *knew* did not end in Reality. Some of the boys began to talk about being ordained, and their interests were in some cases focused on things I con-

sidered to be quite trivial . . . how long must one's surplice be . . .
whose wife could make the most beautiful stoles for the various seasons
of the year—none about which I could care less!

When I had arrived at school I didn't know the *answers* to the
theological questions we were trying to discuss, but I did know the
questions people ask when they're dying and when they are afraid.
And if God through the Church didn't have the answers to these
questions, then how could He be God? I wanted to know how a man
could get to *know* God *personally* in such a way that he could have
something of the Holy Spirit in his life.

I felt that a minister should know God so well that when he came
into someone's living room he could almost sit down quietly and open
his soul in such a way that God's love in his life would create a real
hunger for Reality in the souls of the other people there and lead
them to God too. I sensed intuitively that there must be a way to
introduce God into other people's lives . . . that this must somehow be
what it's all about. But everywhere I found that people wanted to
intellectualize the Good News, wanted to make it conceptual or make
it propositional and in any case to stay away from personal confrontation. And somehow in those intellectualized arguments, the aliveness
of God would evaporate and fade away, only to come back into my
soul when I was alone in prayer.

I studied hard and was as interested as any of them in the academic
work; but I was repelled by the lack of gut-level engagement with the
problems of the rawness of living out one's days and nights as a business
man and husband and citizen. I felt we were dealing with the awesome God of Moses and the Intellectual Power of the Greeks; but
nowhere did I see the personal redeeming God of Jesus Christ.

After four terms of this I realized that whatever it was that was the
matter, (I did not know) I could not in good conscience be ordained.
Mary Allen had had a second baby that fall after my third term. She
almost died following the birth of this baby. She was desperate and
lonely, 1700 miles from home; and I was very little help. I was in a
state of turmoil inside that no one knew about, and I began to fear for
my sanity. I was trying to take care of our two babies and go to classes.
Mary Allen was in the hospital, very sick and frightened. Inside, my

soul was like a tableau of warriors by Michaelangelo, the figures twisting and turning for release. Finally I realized I had to get out of there.
I completed the term; and we left.

The oil company had said we could come back if I ever wanted to
work for them again, and I called. They were very kind, but suddenly
I realized something for the first time: when a young man in our
generation goes off to the ministry, although most of his contemporaries
don't really understand, they think it's fine for him. But when he comes
back, having left the seminary, they don't understand.

Because of my tremendous self-centeredness and pride, I have always
tried desperately to be understood. The oil company took me back
and sent us to an office we had been in before. I would rather have
gone to almost any other place, because this "going back" represented
my first great human failure. There was no way I could explain to the
people around me what had gone on and was going on inside my
soul, behind the confident mask I showed to the world. I began to
work, because I had a wife whom I loved very much and two babies
I loved deeply. But there seemed to be no hope, no ultimate purpose,
anymore. If there was a God, the people at the seminary had subtly
hinted that I must have turned away from Him, (or perhaps this was
my imagination). At any rate I felt things closing in on me in the
inner chamber of my life.

I used to walk down the streets, I remember, and suddenly would
break out in a cold sweat. I thought I might be losing my mind. One
day it was so bad that I got in my company car and took off on a field
trip alone. As I was driving through the tall pine woods country of
East Texas I suddenly pulled up beside the road and stopped. I
remember sitting there in complete despair. I had always been an
optimistic person, and had always had the feeling that there was "one
more bounce in the ball." After a good night's sleep, or perhaps a
couple of martinis and a good night's sleep, one could always start
again tomorrow. But now there was no tomorrow in my situation. I
was like a man on a great gray treadmill going no place, in a world
that was made up of black, black clouds all around me.

As I sat there I began to weep like a little boy, which I suddenly
realized I was inside. I looked up toward the sky. There was nothing

I wanted to do with my life. And I said, "God, if there's anything you want in this stinking soul, take it."

This was almost ten years ago. But something came into my life that day which has never left. There wasn't any ringing of bells or flashing of lights or visions; but it was a deep intuitive realization of what it is God wants from a man, which I had never known before. And the peace which came with this understanding was not an experience in itself, but was rather a cessation of the conflict of a lifetime. I realized then that God does not want a man's money, nor does He primarily want his time, even the whole lifetime of it a young seminarian is ready to give Him. God, I realized, doesn't want your time. He wants your *will;* and if you give Him your will, He'll begin to show you life as you've never seen it before.

It *is* like being born again. I saw that I had not seen Christ at Seminary because I had never known God personally.

As I sat there I continued to cry, only now the tears were a release from a lifetime of being bound by myself, by the terrific drive to prove that I am something—*what* I had never quite understood. Although I could not understand nor articulate for many months what had happened to me, I knew to the core of my soul that I had somehow made personal contact with the very Meaning of Life.

I started the car and turned toward home.

Chapter 4

"... and the two shall become one. This is a great mystery ..."

(Ephesians 5:31-32 RSV)

MARRIAGE
...CHRISTIAN MARRIAGE

To say that life suddenly became a joyous religious dream might make a better story, but life did not. As a matter of fact, my first act after driving home from this commitment encounter was to pour my self a tall scotch and water and think it over. Something had happened to me inside which both frightened and excited me. It was as if my swollen soul had been lanced and the poison drawn out; and I was clean. I had a new chance at life in a way I did not understand but felt deeply to be true. I didn't dare tell my wife for fear she would think I had snapped mentally. When this thought occurred to me I burned my journal describing the hell of the previous months, because I was afraid I *might* be mentally in trouble and this information might be used to have me committed someday. For the first time since I was a child I had a perspective of hope and challenge and completeness . . . a sense of direction.

At that time I remembered when I was a small boy waking up early on Spring mornings and smelling the freshness of the earth and dreaming about those things life might have in store . . . even that day. Then, as I had grown up, I had "put away childish things" and had learned that life was hard and one did not live in continual expectancy. But now, as a grown man with a family, I began waking up and smelling the earth again. I kept waiting for this expectancy to go away, but it never has. Life became animated and real . . . although it began to happen in a way I would never have expected—given my religious preconceptions of what an honestly committed Christian life might be like.

The first inner change I can remember in those beginning months was that I started perceiving things I had never seen before in my own life and in the lives of everyone around me. It was almost as if God had issued me a new set of spiritual eyes. I was both horrified and fascinated at what I saw. For instance, from the time I can remember I had always been trained to be a humble, thoughtful, but hard driving person. I had been kind to people and consciously felt very unworthy of all the little honors and attentions I had received along the way. But later, when I had been married a few months, I noticed that my wife did not see me as the unselfish person other people had intimated I was. In fact she seemed to sense a great deal of *raw selfishness* in my make-up. I was, of course, keenly disappointed—because it was rather obvious to me that Mary Allen (though sweet and loving) was a spoiled and self-centered little girl!

But now suddenly as I looked at my life from this new perspective I saw that all of my goodness and thoughtfulness to people—though consciously sincere for the most part—was a part of my overall life's mission . . . to build an unequaled reputation as a fine successful Christian-type man. Unconsciously I had needed to be right so much that I had paid an amazing price in terms of personal time spent being thoughtful to people. What I now saw which horrified me was that the only thing wrong with my life's plan was that it was (contrary to all my conscious beliefs) *totally self-centered*. It was totally calculated to bring honor to my self . . . though directed toward helping others. I realized with amazement that I am almost a complete egoist.

The next startling discovery I made was that I was basically a coward. This was a real blow; and my mind quickly marshaled dozens of acts and situations which belied this terrible revelation. But I knew it was true, though I had not consciously known before.

With these newly seen facts about myself came the realization that this combination (egoism and cowardice) is not only not uncommon even among Christians in our generation, but is in fact almost a formula for "success" in this country. From the time I was a small boy playing football I can remember tackling boys much larger than myself with great viciousness. My ego was so great that the opinion of the men and boys watching actually meant more to me than my physical well being. I hit hard, not because I was tough—but in order to make sure no one would ever know that down inside I might not want to hit them at all.

In college I didn't stay up all night studying for final examinations because I had an insatiable hunger for a knowledge of economics. I stayed up all night to make sure that I *did not fail.* This combination forces a person to pay the price, whatever it is, for outward success and acclaim . . . but it doesn't make for much of a life inside, behind the mask where we really live. One finds he is always "putting out fires" which might shed light on his true insecurity. But these basic faults in my makeup, even though I had not consciously faced them before, had actually worked to my apparent benefit all my life . . . that is until I got married.

As I have stated, my young wife spotted at least my egoism right away. (It is not difficult to realize whether one's mate's attention is really focused on his or your interest.) I had hidden this self-centeredness so carefully from myself that I would fly into a frustrated and righteous rage when she would come close to revealing it to me. But now after five years of marriage God was letting me see my own life and our marriage in a totally new light. I began to realize that I had never truly known what Christian marriage is. Oh, I could have said some doctrinally correct things about Christian marriage . . . a good many. But I couldn't seem to live them out at our address on a day-in-day-out basis. Now I began to discover existentially some strange things about marriage.

To begin with I saw that in marriage there is shared by the partners something analogous to that inmost secret consciousness in one's own deeply personal experience (which I have called the soul). There is an inner life in a marriage—a life which is lived out when two marriage partners are together with no one else present. This private relationship I shall call the soul of a marriage. And this intimate arena can be more carefully recognized than you might think. There is a specific tone of voice people use. Sometimes a huge booming, business tycoon's voice may take on a whining nasal quality in the intimate encounter with his wife in the soul of their marriage. The pillar of the "women of the church" who is all sweetness and light to the outer world, may turn into a hissing caustic hussy in the private arena of her marriage. There is a definite and highly communicative language marriage partners share at this level in their relationship—much of it unspoken. Each partner has a whole repertoire of "glances." A woman has her "angry" look; a man has his "I hate your guts" look. Or there is the "you're drinking too much, George" look. I have seen a woman nail her husband with a silent glance thirty feet across a crowded cocktail party . . . and watched him wilt as they shared the message intimately in the soul of their marriage . . . surrounded by a hundred oblivious people. The soul of a marriage can be a trysting place where two people can come together quietly from the struggles of the world and feel safe, accepted, and loved . . . or it can be a battle ground where two egos are locked in a lifelong struggle for supremacy, a battle which is for the most part invisible to the rest of the world.

Another thing about this area of married life is that we soon place some articles of "furniture" in the soul of a marriage: some resentments, some jealousy, some situations which can be counted on unfailingly to bring anguish. These things begin to clutter up the soul of a marriage almost from the first night.

With this picture of the inner marriage life in mind, the basic practical problem of a marriage now seems to me to be this: two fine healthy young people wake up one morning and find themselves alone together in the soul of their marriage . . . realizing that they really don't know each other at all. What has happened is that each partner has come into the marriage with his own vision of what a marriage ought to be.

A girl's vision of a husband depends on many things—what her father was like (and whether she idolized him or despised him), what novels she has read, what movies she has seen. All of her impressions of the ideal man for her, unconsciously for the most part, go into a composite image which she dreams her marriage partner will fulfill. A man's vision of a wife evolves in a similar fashion. In retrospect I think Mary Allen's vision of a husband was a perfectly balanced blend of Big John Wayne, Jack Parr and Father Flanagan. But in all honesty I think my pre-marital vision of an ideal wife was probably a combination of St. Theresa, Elizabeth Taylor and . . . Betty Crocker. But, of course, a wife not only has a vision of what a husband should be like, she also has a vision of what a *wife* should be. Any similarity between the husband's vision of an ideal wife and the wife's vision of an ideal wife is a rare and beautiful coincidence.

These different visions of the roles of each partner in a marriage constitute a good bit of the material for the frustrating struggles in the soul of the marriage. Many times the girl may have seen some basic difference in her vision of a husband and the actual man she is about to marry. But the aura of romance (or the unusual confidence of American women) makes her feel that she can change the actual man to fit the mental image, thus making her total acceptance of him *conditional* . . . a fact which though unconscious to her becomes apparent to the husband quickly in a marriage's soul. Besides this, the young man may have been counting on the wife's changing to his vision. So what do we have?—*two* creators, *two gods,* in the soul of one marriage . . . each vying, each insisting on the validity of his own created image of what a husband and wife, what a marriage ought to be.

So the invisible battle lines are drawn across the soul of a marriage and the siege begins. This is not to say that there is not a great deal of happiness (physical and otherwise) in such a marriage. But in its soul there is at best a peaceful co-existence between two wills, a sort of stalemate with little pockets of resentment and hurt.

This is, I am convinced, an X-ray picture of many marriages within the leadership groups of Protestant Churches in every city. And although the first five years of our marriage were, I had thought, the happiest of any couple I knew, the above description in many respects was a picture of our marriage from my perspective. For five years our relationship had been a good one with a lot of happiness and love and with a reasonably workable truce in its soul with regard to the battle of the wills. But our visions of marriage differed in several important respects.

For one thing, my wife had been raised in a family with five daughters and no sons. Her father was of the old Southern school and didn't believe in men helping around the house with dishes, etc. But he made one concession in that he would take the trash basket in the kitchen out and empty it each evening for Mary Allen's mother. I had been raised with only one brother. My father was also of the old Southern background and he did not believe in helping with little household chores either . . . *especially* things like emptying the *trash basket*. And so when we got married and came home from our honeymoon, Mary Allen announced happily, "Honey, unlike some of my friends I don't want you to dry the dishes and mop the floors or make beds. These things are woman's work." I was about to pop with pride and thanksgiving, when she continued, "But I would appreciate it if you would take the trash basket in the kitchen out and empty it in the evenings."

I was stunned. I realized this was a very crucial point affecting my vision of a man and a husband.

"Honey, I'm sorry," I said slowly, "but I'm *not* taking out that waste basket. That's woman's work."

Now *she* was stunned . . . and a little angry.

"That's *all* I'm asking you to do!" she said in amazement.

"Honey, I'll work at night and *hire* someone to help you," I said determinedly, "but I'm not taking out that waste basket." So the waste basket in the kitchen became the first article of furniture in the soul of our marriage, which had to be stepped around almost daily in our relationship: (Don't laugh, your marriage must have something like this. Maybe it's the toothpaste tube—you may be a "roller" and she's a "squeezer.")

Another thing that characterized our marriage relationship was the overwhelming percentage of the instances in which I was deeply convinced that I was right, when we had arguments. I always had a justification for everything I did. Oh, I had given in all right—for strategic reasons—but I had felt very big about doing so.

With all of these little things, however, we had a fine marriage. I suppose (in retrospect) we were just trying to take the rough edges off of each other in the soul of our marriage . . . with sandpaper. But then, five years later, I had gotten to the end of my mental rope that day beside the road in East Texas.

Then as I began to see the enormity of my ego and the subtlety of my selfishness, I soon had to bring this new perspective and knowledge into the soul of our marriage.

It happened like this: We were arguing about something (not long after I had tried to offer my life to God) and at the height of the disagreeing Mary Allen shook her head and said (as she had a thousand times) in that discouraged tone I knew so well, "Honey, you are *wrong!*"

Ordinarily this would only have spurred me on to further justification of my point. But this time I stopped and thought about what she was trying to tell me. After a few seconds I said slowly, "Honey, I believe you are right. I think I *am* wrong."

Amazed, she looked at me cautiously to see if something sarcastic was coming; and when it didn't, she said a little confused, "Wait a minute, maybe *I'm* wrong."

This may not sound like much to you. But it was the beginning of a whole new kind of life in the intimate soul of our marriage. For the first time I didn't need so desperately to be right . . . to be the victorious hero in all the encounters in our relationship. I could relax and begin to be myself. I suppose this new commitment idea I was trying to live would have been all right with my wife (she certainly liked the changes in me) . . . except for one horrible mistake I made: I tried to convince her that *she* should do the same thing. On the surface it sounds perfectly logical that a husband who has been deeply converted to a Living Christ should go about trying to get his wife equally converted. I am convinced that this is not only wrong, but that it is one of the unnecessary sources of deepest anguish in marriages in which only one partner is really trying to commit his life to Christ.

From *my* perspective I was trying to tell Mary Allen that I had found something wonderful—a freedom and sense of reality I'd never known was possible for people like us. But strangely, my most enthusiastic witnessing made her very cool and upset. I couldn't understand it. Later she told me that from *her* perspective all she could hear me saying those days beneath my words was that we had been happily married for five years and now suddenly I didn't like her as she was. I was not going to accept her fully anymore unless she *changed* into some kind of religious fanatic (or changed somehow in a way she didn't know how to change). I was threatening her very life and our life together . . . and of course I didn't even realize it, since I was saying such "good, true things." So, in her rebellion, she had begun subtly to point to areas in my life wherein if I were such a committed Christian, why was it that I "still reacted in the same old way"?

In my frustration I began to try to convince her that God had really changed me. In looking around for something to do to prove that I had changed I did as many well meaning Christians do when they are trying to convince someone close to them that they are different. I fastened onto something *I* liked to do. I decided to be more loving.

There is nothing wrong with being more loving . . . except that at the time it made me happier instead of her. A dear friend of ours in New York finally brought home the stark fallacy of my secret campaign by telling me what his wife used to do when she wanted to convince him that she was a good Christian wife or that she was sorry for some selfish behavior. She would bake him a pie. She loved to bake and was a terrific cook. The only trouble was that my friend didn't like pies;—he wanted her to make love to him.

While I was looking around for some other way to convince my wife that I had really changed, my glance fell on the waste basket standing full by the back door. "No, Lord," I groaned quietly to myself, "*Not* the waste basket. Take my income, anything." But I suddenly knew that for me it had to be the wastebasket. Without saying a word I took it out, and didn't even mention it to her. (I had emptied it before in order to manipulate her into doing something I wanted to do. But not this time.) I began to really make an effort to take the trash out every day because I realized *that this was where my pride was fastened.* And I think this was when Mary Allen knew that something had really happened in my soul. I learned through this experience to look at the grubby little resentments and in areas where I am deeply defending my position to find really convincing ways to express the selfless love of Christ in my intimate human relationships with those people who truly know me.

Finally I realized the un-Christian pressure my trying to force Mary Allen into my version of a Christian wife was having in her life. We were drifting further and further apart. Although things looked happy on the surface, we both knew that our marriage was bruised and broken on the inside where the world could not see. Finally one night

I said to her, "Honey, I can't deny the tremendous things which have happened to me these past two years because of trying to give my future to the finding of God's will. But I have been wrong in trying to force all this on you. No one forced it on me. I'm sorry I tried (however unconsciously) to manipulate you by taking you to all these meetings etc. to get you converted. I am really sorry." I went on to tell her, "When we got married I didn't sign up to *change* you, just to *love* you . . . and I do, just as you are."

This took the pressure off her, because I really meant it. Within a few weeks she went out and made a beginning commitment of her future to Christ all by herself, in the way which was right for her. (And it almost hurt my feelings that it didn't happen through me, but through a friend.) How wrong I have been so many times in these past few years in trying to change people instead of loving them. I believe we delude ourselves in thinking we can change people anyway. I am convinced that only God can convert anyone.

What happens when God's will becomes personally real and important to both parties in a Christian marriage? Then for the first time a Christian home is a live option. Now in the soul of our marriage it was not *my* vision of what a marriage or husband should be against *her* vision—one of us always having to be wrong. But now, together we began trying to find out Christ's vision of what our marriage should be.

I found that in a Christian home the husband was to be the spiritual head (I Cor. 11:3). This implied making some decisions which I had never made. The wife is to look to the husband for strength and authority under God (Eph. 5:22f.). I had been straining so hard to make our home a democracy because of my insecurity that she had never been able to look to me for these things really. But now that we both wanted a Christian home we began to try to live together in a new way. The awful sniping at each other wasn't necessary to gain supremacy points or get even. We could afford to admit we were wrong and help and accept each other with all of our faults, because we began to feel deeply accepted by God, even though we were seeing our selfishness more and more as we looked toward Christ.

For the first five years of our marriage I had been trying somehow to prove to Mary Allen that I was a "man"; and finally I could admit (she already knew of course) that I am only a little boy trying to impress the world that I am a man. At last we can relax and be children in the soul of our marriage and find peace together.

All of this does not imply that a Christian marriage is one with no problems or even a marriage with fewer problems. (It may well mean *more* problems.) But it does mean a life in which two people are able to accept each other and love each other in the *midst* of problems and fears. It means a marriage in which selfish people can accept selfish people without constantly trying to change them—and even accept themselves, because they realize personally that they have been accepted by Christ . . . by God. And they are involved together in the adventure of trying to find God's will for their lives.

In honesty I must say that I am still an egoist and still a coward; but now, because of God's amazing gift of His presence and the perception which comes through beginning to give one's life to Him with no strings, I can sometimes live and make decisions in my own personal life as if I were not these things. And believe me that is Good News!

Chapter 5

"Thy will be done,
On earth as it is in Heaven."

(Matthew 6:10 RSV)

A LIFE WITH PRAYER

All of my life I have been looking for a sense of completeness in my soul. I have done a great deal of nervous talking about what I would like to do with my life. And I have sent up dozens if not hundreds of urgent prayers for guidance. I have studied. I have competed in business and socially. I have jumped in and espoused safe causes in the church. But all of my turning from one thing to another, my fantastic searching, had left me exhausted and afraid that there was no peace, no real continuity of purpose and direction for a man in his soul.

And then it had come . . . the falling into place of all the pieces of the puzzle—not intellectually, but intuitionally. How can one describe this integrating conformation of meaning to life, this release from that many-headed monster: the fear of unfulfillment, hiding somewhere in the darkness ahead?

When I was a small boy we lived in a two story house near the edge of town. One day I was playing alone in my parent's bedroom upstairs. I was sitting on the floor, completely absorbed, playing with some toy soldiers, a brass tray, and a large battered tablespoon, among other things. Suddenly I looked up and realized I was totally alone in the house. I remember the throbbing silence. The aloneness terrified me and I began to sing and beat on the brass tray with the battered tablespoon, somehow feeling that if I could only keep up the noise nothing would creep up and get me. I remember being afraid to shout "Mother" for fear it (whatever it was that was going to get me) might know I was frightened and come out of its hiding place. The terror was agony; and I remember singing at the top of my lungs and beating the brass tray with huge tears streaming down my face and my heart about to jump out of my chest. When at last my mother came in from the back yard and came upstairs, I can still remember the feeling of exhaustion and the tears of relief as I collapsed into her arms and was released from my self-made prison of noise and fear.

I think something that "felt" like this took place in that first attempt to surrender my will to God by the roadside. But it was *more* than emotion. Martin Buber has tried to describe what happens to a man when he encounters God personally. He says, "Man receives and he receives not a 'specific content' but a Presence, a Presence as power."[1] He is bound up in a new relation. Now this is no lightheaded release from the responsibility of intelligent thought "nor does it in any way lighten his life—it makes his life heavier, but heavy with meaning" . . . . "there is the inexpressible conformation of meaning. Meaning is assured. Nothing can any longer be meaningless. The question about the meaning of life is no longer there. But were it there, it would not have to be answered. You do not know how to exhibit and define the meaning of life, you have no formula nor picture for it, and yet it has more certitude for you than the perception of your senses."[2] This was true for me as I set out to try to live my life for Jesus Christ.

But one of the first things I came to realize was that I didn't know how to begin to find God's will for me particularly. I had always rather naively assumed that the making of a "total commitment" sort of automatically ushered into one's experience a vital prayer life (whatever that meant) and ushered out the preoccupation with old resentments or thoughts of sleeping with one of the secretaries at the office or one's friends' wives. But this was not the case for me.

I have always pictured my inner life as a sort of cavern inside my head out of which I look at you, the rest of the world, through my eyes in the wall of the cavern. This cavern has a pool of liquid filling it about two-thirds full. The part above the surface of the pool is my

1. Martin Buber, *I and Thou*, New York: Charles Scribner's Sons, 1958, p. 110.
2. *Ibid.*

conscious life and the larger part, beneath the surface where I cannot see, is my unconscious life. The day I decided to commit my life wholly to God, I scooped up everything I could see above the level of consciousness and offered it to Christ. I felt free; but then, several mornings later a hoary head came up out of the slimy pool, an old resentment.

I was filled with discouragement and I thought I must not have really committed my life to God at all. But then I realized joyously that of course I had—that all a man does when he commits his "whole life" is to commit that of which he is conscious. And according to many psychologists, the major part of the human Psyche is below the level of consciousness.[3] So the totally "committed" Christian life is a life of continually committing one's self and problems day by day as they are slowly revealed to his own consciousness. I think many Christians have become discouraged or given up because they have at some time made a new beginning with God and then found their minds filled with lust, resentment, and jealousy. Discouraged, they have assumed that they are not in right relationship with God at all. Naturally they do not want to admit these problems in their Sunday School classes, since they assume the rest of us are not plagued with such horrible and unchristian thoughts.

But since I now wanted to commit my future to God, I had to find out *specific* ways to align my rebellious and wavering will to His. I had always "prayed" sporadically; but my prayer life was a rather mechanical monologue. I had prayed about *big* things (cancer, success, deliverance) but didn't want to disturb God over the *little* problems of every day living (resentment, jealousy, slothfulness). Now suddenly I realized that there are no small decisions—since every deciding either takes one closer to or further from God's will.

In order to develop a fulfilling prayer life, I had tried books of prayer, reading Psalms and all sorts of devotional books. But again and again I wound up praying something like: "Dear God, forgive me for all the bad things I do. Help me to be better; thank you for all the many blessings you have given me; and help everybody everywhere."

3. See Jolande Jacobi's *The Psychology of C. G. Jung*, New Haven: Yale University Press, 1962, Chapter 1, p. 5f.

That prayer seemed to pretty well cover everything, but nothing much *happened* in my life. Then people began to tell me I needed to have a certain period of time each day for private prayer. I tried that . . . and failed, again and again, to get up that few minutes before everyone else did in the mornings.

I can remember the alarm going off those mornings (very early). I would wake up and force myself to my feet to feel around in the dark for my robe and slippers in the closet or for my Bible in the blackness. If I couldn't find everything right away, I would tell God sleepily, "Lord, you know it is not fair for me to wake up my family (who need their sleep) just to satisfy my selfish desire to have a time of prayer. Deliver me from that kind of legalism." And I'd go back to bed.

Or I can remember waking up early on cold winter mornings after a late night up and saying, "Lord, you know how unreasonable I am with my family when I don't get enough sleep. And since you have made it clear to me recently that I should be more thoughtful of them, I'm going to sleep this morning . . . knowing . . . you will . . . understand."

Or I can remember other times when I have awakened and decided to pray in bed in that semi-drowsy, half-conscious state (when the will is disengaged). These times certainly felt "spiritual," but they are not, I learned, to be confused with Christian prayer.

Nothing seemed to be working and I knew there was something really missing in my prayer life. Finally one day I met a layman whose life had a power and a concern in it which I knew instinctively were the things my Christian life desperately lacked. Everywhere this man went he left in his wake business men and women who began to be different people and whose lives became disciplined and focused on the Living God. I asked this man what he considered to be most important in the discipline of his Christian life. He pointed out that reading the Scriptures every day and having a specific time of prayer for the cultivation of a real and dynamic relationship with Christ were the two things which had become most meaningful and real to him.

Seeing a *life* with which I could identify did for me what all my "trying" could not—motivated me to begin a regular time of prayer and devotional reading of the Bible each day. I began, and through faith in another man's faith, was able to continue through the dry periods until now this time has become the center from which I live the rest of my life.

At this point things began to change. I realized that if Christianity is a living relationship with God I had to find out what this God is really like to whom I had committed my future. I realized that my closest relationships had always been with those who knew the most about me, and loved me anyway. So I began to reveal my inner life to Him, all of it (even though I knew He already knew). This experience taught me the strange power in prayer of being *specific* with God. After making as total and complete a confession of all of the moral weaknesses and specific sins I could recall, I thanked him for His forgiveness. I began to examine myself daily and "keep short accounts with God."

In trying to be totally honest I found a new freedom and sense of being accepted. For now I didn't psychologically need to gloss over my true greed and lust and excuse it as being insignificant. I knew I was accepted. Instead of saying "Lord, today I exaggerated a little on my expense account, but you know everyone does." I was able to say, "Lord, I *cheated* on my expense account to-day. Help me not to be a dirty thief." Or instead of saying, "Lord, I couldn't help noticing that secretary down the hall . . . it was such a windy day . . . but Lord you know that boys will be boys," I began to be able to level with God and to say openly to him, "Lord, I thought of sleeping with that girl in my imagination. This is the kind of man I am. Forgive me and give me the power and the desire to be different."

As I read passages like First John 1:9 I began to really believe that God could forgive me and would. And my desires began to change. Things began to be different not only in my devotional time but in my whole day. In looking for *specific* things to thank God for each morning I began to see His hand everywhere, and life became richer and filled with good things.

For a long time I had been disturbed about the problem of a wandering mind during my time of prayer. I would be trying to pray and suddenly my mind would jump to a business appointment I needed to make. For years I had forced these things out of my mind to get back to "spiritual things." But now, thanks to another Christian friend, I began to keep a list by my side; and when the thought came to me to call someone, to make an appointment, or to do something for the family, I began to jot it down and then go back to God. I was at last realizing that He is interested in my total life and that these things which came into my mind during my time of prayer might be significant things for me to do, or places for me to go. This also made it easier for me to get my mind immediately back to my other prayers.

Sometimes a vision of someone I resented would come floating into my prayers or some incongruous situation that I did not want to think about. Instead of suppressing it, I began to offer the person or the thing immediately to God in prayer, asking Him to make my thoughts about this person more like His. I began to keep a list of people for whom I wanted to pray. And before I knew it, I discovered that God was touching more and more of my life through this time of prayer. I realized experimentally that the Incarnation means that God has made the material world of people and things His concern and that we must make it our concern for Him.

But there was a fly in the ointment. I found that although I had believed God could forgive me for all my selfishness and sins, I discovered that I could not forgive myself for one of them in particular. After months of inner anguish and continued confusion I was talking to a close Christian friend. In a prayer I confessed this sin aloud to God before this friend. And within a few days, I could accept God's forgiveness. As a Protestant I had always been repelled (and frightened) at the idea of revealing my true self before another person. But now I realized why Luther made the admonition in James to "confess your sins to one another" (James 5:16) a part of the Priesthood of all believers.[4]

This experience opened a whole area of my Christian life. I realized that once a man has confessed his most awful sins to God *before another person*, he can never again pretend (comfortably) that he is righteous . . . however famous he may become as a Christian. He can quit wasting so much of his energy explaining himself and making sure that everyone understands that he is a good man. Because now he

4. Martin Luther, Works, V. 36, p. 86.

knows that at least one other fallible human being knows that he is not. He is a selfish sinner. I am not recommending this to anyone. I am merely saying that *I* was trapped with some terrible anguish; and through this kind of specific confessing with a trusted friend (whom I knew might fail me), I found myself in a position in which I had to trust God with my reputation . . . and I found a new freedom. I could begin to be my true self with other people, realizing that as awful as I am, Christ loved me enough to die for me and people like me. Now I really *wanted* to be different in my life *out of gratitude*.

At this point a new honesty crept into my prayers. Before this, I had always started out by saying "God, I adore you" (whether I really did or not that morning). Now I could say, (when it was true), "Lord, I am sorry but I am tired of you today. I am tired of trying to do your will all of the time, and I'd like to run away and raise hell." But now I could also continue; "But, Lord, forgive me for this willfulness: and even though I don't 'feel like' it, I ask you to lead me today to be your person and to do your will." This was a real act of *faith*, because there was no religious feeling involved. My days began to take on the character of adventure.

Howard Butt, Jr. has been a tremendous help to me at this point. He once told me about waking up one morning and beginning a time of prayer only to find that he was as stale and flat as he could be. He couldn't sense God's presence at all. But he said, "God, I thank you for being with me even though I don't *feel* as if you are within a thousand miles." When he said this, I at once thought it sounded like some kind of auto-suggestion; but he continued and said, "Lord, I believe you are here, not because I feel like it, but I believe it on faith in the authority of your Word. You said you would be with us." As he continued I realized that in so much of my life I had been a spiritual sensualist, always wanting to *feel* God's presence in my prayers and being depressed when I didn't. I saw that until I could believe *without* spiritual goose pimples I would always be vacillating, and my faith would be at the mercy of my emotional feelings. So I tried this praying whether I felt spiritual or not; and for the first time in my life found that we *can* live on raw faith. I found that often the very act of praying this way brings later a closer sense of God's Presence. And I realized a strange thing: that if a person in his praying has the *feeling*, he doesn't really need the *faith*. I began to feel very tender toward God on those mornings during which I would pray without any conscious sense of His Presence. I felt this way because at last I was giving back to Him the gift of faith.

Things began to change more rapidly in my inner life. It wasn't that I got rid of all my problems (as many Christian witnesses and evangelists seem to imply, thus making us all feel guilty and inadequate when we have problems). But I simply began getting a *new set* of problems. I came to realize that God wasn't going to take things out of my life. Instead He *brought in* a great many positive new things. Since my life and my time were already filled to overflowing, some things had to go . . . but He made *me* choose what they would be. And it was a great day when I found my whole set of values and my honest secret inner desires were changing. In a life of faith, I discovered, "renunciation is not sacrifice."[5] I had read and now saw the truth in the late Mahatma Gandhi's statement: "Only give up a thing when you want some other condition so much that the thing has no longer any attraction for you, *or* when it seems to interfere with that which is more greatly desired."[6] At first I had thought that if this were true I was stuck with some of my problems for life. But now I found that this advice was actually becoming true in my own prayer life. I began to *want* to be Christ's person enough to pray that He would reveal to me those thoughts and habits which were standing between Him and me and my doing His will. I prayed that He would then give me the desire and the power to change.

Right here I ran into a problem that is very subtle even among the ranks of the newly committed disciples of our Lord. That problem was this: for years I had been engaged in a conformity to the social and economic world. This conformity had influenced the kind of clothes I wore and the kind of house I lived in, etc. But now having recognized this conformity to the world, I was tempted to trade it (unconsciously)

---

5. Louis Fischer, *Ghandi, His Life and Message for the World*, New York: Mentor Books, 1960, p. 34.

6. *Ibid.*, See Christian expression of this experience reflected in the 14th chapter of Romans.

for a conformity with the prevailing opinions of my new Christian friends concerning my behavior. In other words, as I prayed that God would reveal any changes I should make in my life, I was at the same time being pressured from the outside to make changes by Christian friends who were slightly appalled at some of my activities as a "good Christian". I am convinced that the changing of your behavior for *any* reason other than that of honestly believing that *Christ* would have you change it leaves the door open to all kinds of cliquish spiritual pride and self-righteousness (regardless of whether or not the change itself is good).

But how does one actually go about deciding to change his social and ethical behavior as a committed Christian? And having decided, how does one carry out these changes without being a pious fraud? Several years ago I might have thought that these questions were out of place in a discussion on a life of prayer. But if a Christian life is one of praise and adoration and the conforming of one's life and the world around him to the purposes and will of God, then I realized that a life of prayer to have any fiber or reality about it had better also deal with the areas yet unchanged.

One of the things God brought into my already full life as a young business man was the desire to tell other people that life wasn't a hopeless rat race, to tell them the Good News. This led to my beginning to teach an adult Sunday School class. Because many of the members of this class were college professors with advanced degrees, my intense pride demanded a great deal of study and preparation for Sunday morning. As I began to study about ten hours a week for my thirty minute talk on Sunday morning, several things began to demand change.

We had often stayed out late on Saturday nights, going to dinners, movies, dances . . . mostly involving some preparatory social drinking, some sustaining social drinking and/or some later "one for the road" social drinking. But as I began to go home and try to put the finishing touches on my Sunday School lesson at 2:30 a.m. some Sunday mornings, I realized that just as a practical matter if nothing else, some changes were in order. So we started coming in earlier. When we began to reserve Sunday as a family day with the children, we found that we felt terrible physically after a late evening with too much to eat or drink. I discovered that in order to be a loving parent and thoughtful husband (which I now really wanted to be) I needed more sleep than I was getting anyway. So I began to *want* to live a life with more order and moderation in it enough to see how we could have one. And the subsequent changes in our social life opened a whole new world of personal relationships and family activities I had never before "had time for."

All this time, while I was praying for God to reveal His will to me, I was being confronted in my soul with relationships which needed changing, attitudes toward my family, my work, Negroes, sexual lust, the magazines I was reading, my lack of involvement in politics as a Christian, and a good many other things which brought me to my knees continually in frustration mixed with the joy of knowing that God was changing my perspective and desires. He was giving me the power to occasionally be at least intellectually the free man I had always wanted to be in these areas.

As I continued to pray and read the New Testament, I learned that Christ's criteria for a Godly life were not doctrinal as ours so often are. His had to do with allegiance to Himself and the *fruits* that allegiance produced in a man's *relationships with other men.* (John 1:12 NEB; Matthew 7:15f; 11:2f; 12:33; 25:31f; Luke 10:29-37 etc.) And I began to see that a life of prayer is to be judged ultimately not so much by even our devotion in praying and witnessing and inner moral rectitude as by whether or not we have fed the hungry, clothed the naked and loved the loveless stranger (Matthew 25:31f). It dawned on me with a sudden jolt that real prayer, Christian prayer, inevitably drives a man, sooner or later, out of the privacy of his soul, beyond the circle of his little group of Christian friends and *across the barriers between social, racial and economic strata to find the wholeness, the real closeness of Christ in that involvement with the lives of His lost and groping children whoever and wherever they may be.*

But behind and woven through all of these outer problems and adjustments had developed a new inner prayer life. There was a sense of active adventure. My prayers were no longer vague mystical "feelings." I was communicating with a God who was *alive*, about real issues and real people in my days and nights. God was trying to give me an abundant new experience of life, when and if I would take it . . . . a day, an hour at a time. When my regular morning prayers would start out "dry" I learned to read devotional books (like *My Utmost for His Highest* by Oswald Chambers or *The Imitation of Christ* by Thomas á Kempis) to turn my thoughts toward Him, toward Christ. Then I had found that by following any such reading with a passage from the New Testament every day I was gradually filling my unconscious life with God's message. And as I was revealing myself to Him in confession, He was revealing His character and purposes to me through the reading again of the way Christ reacted throughout the story of His life, death, and resurrection and of His spirit in the formation and development of the early Church.

I began to see as I never had the relationship of my prayer life to my physical and emotional life. A large glass of hot water and a few minutes of regular exercises just before one's prayer time each morning can change the whole climate of one's relationship with God and with other people.[7] Because we are to come to Him with our whole lives . . . not just our "spirit."

I have learned to love Christ personally. For now we have been through almost ten years of struggles and failures and joys together in the privacy of my soul and on the outer stage of my life. I have come to want to find new ways to praise Him for giving me a sense of unity, of wholeness, in my life. All of the different personalities I had projected in the various areas of my experience were somehow being melded into one. I didn't have to have a separate vocabulary, a different kind of humor and a different set of ethics for my business life, my church life, my family life, and my prayer life. It was as if Christ had taken his fist and begun to knock out the partitions in my soul which had made my life so fragmented.

Finally, I began to see that prayer is not a series of requests to get God to help me do things I think need to be done. Prayer is a direction

---

7. For an excellent set of apparently safe, graduated exercises for men and women, see booklet produced for the Canadian Air Force: *Royal Canadian Air Force Exercise Plans for Physical Fitness*, 630 Fifth Ave., New York Pocket Books, Inc.

of life, a focusing of one's most personal and deepest attention God-ward. The purpose is to love God and learn to know Him so well, that our wills, our actions will be more and more aligned with His, until even our unconscious reactions and purposes will have the mark of His love, His life about them. Prayer was no longer an 'activity.' It had become the continuing language of that relationship God designed to fulfill a human life. But about this time I found that I simply couldn't live it alone.

Chapter 6

"... woe to him who is alone when he falls and has not another to lift him up."

(Ecclesiastes 4:10 RSV)

GROUPS FOR STRUGGLERS

At this point in my pilgrimage I could identify with Christian in *Pilgrim's Progress* when he had seen the cross and had had the burden of his separation lifted from his life but was really only beginning his journey. I was experiencing a new kind of life. In perceiving the trap of my own self-centeredness I could also see others trapped in theirs and could love them and want them to find the freedom I was beginning to find. I had begun to *listen* to Mary Allen and the children and other people in my life, really listen to what they were saying. I had begun to try to see what their dreams and frustrations were as people. At church I had begun teaching a class with many apparently interested people in it. But here I was stymied. I knew God was real and knew He was doing miracles in my own home. But I was having a terrible time communicating the things I knew experientially to be true to other members of the church I attended. The people in the Sunday School class seemed to accept me and believe what I told them; but their lives were not changing. At least they were not changing in any way observable to me. I found that by myself I kept losing the perspective and the vision of Christ's purposes, and I was frustrated.

Out of my own loneliness and discouragement I decided to ask a few people to begin meeting with me one night a week for an eight week's trial period. My first inclination was to ask some of the "other" leaders of the church. My thinking being that if *they* would see this new life, the whole town might come alive. But to my surprise they

were almost all too busy with meetings etc. to want to come. So I
thought about Christ and what He did. Then I decided that I would
look around the church and find eleven or twelve people who seemed
most hungry to know God, whoever they might be. I found a couple
who were dear friends who had just lost a child, a divorcee, a young
man getting ready to go to seminary, a couple who had no children, a
woman who had come into the Episcopal Church from the Roman
Catholic Church recently, a man who sold heavy road equipment and
one couple in the building business with four children. I went to see
these people individually and told them what was happening in my life
and asked them if they would like to meet with other people who were
seeking to know Christ. The only criterion for joining the group was
that each of the people had to *want* to give his life to God (even
though he might not be able to do it).

The small groups in my past church experience had provided no
answer per se; and many times they had degenerated into cliques,
gossip sessions or debating societies. So this time we decided that the
clear purpose was to be: getting to know the Living Christ. We were
not going to argue about the *existence* of God, but were going to try
to find out how each of us might get to *know* Him personally as He is
revealed in Jesus Christ.

We decided to make an experiment with each one of our lives during that period and to report back to the group each week concerning
our failures, our joys, and the ridiculous things which happened to us
as we tried to take Christ consciously through the routine of our days
and nights. We made it sort of a secretive thing . . . like an under-
ground experiment. And we came back to each meeting with an excitement as we began to see how strangely timid and insecure we were
in our faith. We could laugh at ourselves and vicariously experience
through each other the fears and joys and insights of a life with Christ
in the center of it.

We divided the time into three sections during those evenings. As
we shared the problems and discoveries of that week we began to see
together the fresh and contemporary footprints of Christ through our
lives. We studied the Bible. Most of the people never really had and
admitted that they were ashamed of how little they knew about the

content of the Bible. And we spent the last part of the evening praying together.

As those eight weeks grew into two years, and as we studied the Bible and shared our own real lives, we found that we had never really known each other at all before the group started. We found that we had not been able to communicate because we were basically afraid of each other somehow and did not know how to reveal our true selves without being embarrassed.

After about two years one of our ministers came to me (I had talked to him about the group prior to its beginning, which I strongly recommend doing) and asked me what I was telling the group about financial stewardship. I tried to think, and realized that we had never talked about giving, as such. The minister wondered because several of the people in the group had obviously begun to tithe and all of our personal giving to the church had increased considerably. I began to get excited as I realized what was happening to us as individuals apart from our time together each week. Several of the people had become church school teachers, one the superintendent of the Sunday School, one had become head of the Women of the Church and had so loved the group that she had been appointed area director of Episcopal Women's work for a large part of the state. Three of us had been elected to the vestry of the church. And all of us had found new life in our own church experience. Because now we had something to talk about. Christ was not a distant figure but through the Holy Spirit He was becoming alive in our midst. We felt a different kind of love for each other, for other people, and for Him. I realized that these were the things our Vestries and Christian Education Committees had been concentrating on for years. We had found them to be only the *by-products* of getting to know the Living Christ together.

Now my own inner life had taken on a whole new dimension. I was not alone in it. The group became a spiritual family to come back to with my failures and successes. My whole concept of group leadership suddenly had taken a change. I can remember the strange paradox as "group leader" when the group finally came alive. In the beginning Mary Allen had been skeptical about having a regular gathering of people with different backgrounds in terms of age, marital status, social habits and interests together and hoping for any kind of common ground. But I felt that these were the people whom God had given us. And besides, if it failed nothing would be hurt but my pride. I wasn't selling anything; so we tried it.

Things went pretty smoothly until about the third meeting. To put us all on a more equal basis and to force us to examine the Scriptures for ourselves no one was allowed to use the Bible Commentaries until *after* a session in which the passage was discussed. This saved the people from the anxiety of expressing an honest opinion for fear the leader had *the* answer and was ready to pounce on them with it.

But about the third meeting, I expressed an opinion about the meaning of the passage, and two of the members of the group heartily disagreed. A third took up their position. We checked the passage for study in the secondary sources for the next week, and the meeting ended. As it turned out they were right and I was wrong. I felt sick. I had been so sure that I was right. I felt that I had failed them as a leader and that they would lose confidence in me and the group would disintegrate. I told all this to Mary Allen and was reconciled to my failure. But during that week one member of the group after another called, filled with enthusiasm, telling me they thought that at last the group was coming alive and that that meeting had meant more to them than any of the others.

Right then two thoughts struck me: (1) That a Christian leader must die in a sense to his own image of perfection that others may live. Now the people realized I was just one of them and that they too were first class citizens and not just "my group." My being wrong and their being able to help me did something for all of us. I quit having the pressure to be right all of the time as leader and relaxed. They gained a new kind of group confidence and freedom. (2) It hit me that when the group leader is in control and things "feel good" to him about a meeting, it is not necessarily good from the participants' perspective. Many times the leader's very painful experience of "laying down his life for his friends" in witnessing to his own failure and being vulnerable makes for an exciting and joyous breakthrough for the *rest* of the group. This seeing *them* come alive and gain confidence was paradoxically a far greater joy than having a "successful group" as a smooth leader. This was true even though my pride seemed to be taking all kinds of blows.

As the months had gone by and we had met in each other's homes to pray and talk about Jesus Christ, our homes became more natural places to talk about Him during other nights of the week. We began to learn vicariously through each other's experiences. One of us would tell the group: "I have a neighbor who has been mean to our children for years, and I've despised her. Now I find that we have been elected President and Vice-President of the P.T.A. What can I do to let her know that I now love her? The two of us have a meeting set for tomorrow." Then someone else in the group who had recently faced resentment in his own life would witness to his own struggle; and out of this dialogue often concrete suggestions came to us which we might not have stumbled onto alone for years because of our lack of perspective, each being so close to his own problems.

As time went on I found that I desperately needed the balance, correction, and love of such a group. The openness and acceptance helped me more and more to be honest—not only with the group but in my business life and at home. The fresh witness of lives being changed before one's eyes brings a perpetual newness and wonder when your own experience gets flabby and gray.

I will never forget a young couple, whom I shall call Betty and Joe, who were a part of a later group. One night Betty came into the group. She was very attractive and had three lovely small children; but she told us (later) that her marriage was on the ropes. She was a very vivacious party-girl type who did the twist and told shocking stories to mixed groups. She had been a church-goer for years but now, out of a deep need she came and gave herself as wholly to Christ as she knew how. And her life began to change in a marked way. I remember eight weeks later she was leading us in a period of prayer. Afterwards she said quietly to the group, "You know, all my life I've been trying to get your attention, I have showed off, told risque stories, and done all kinds of things to get you to notice me, to love me." She paused and then continued, "And when you didn't, I gossiped about you, cut you to ribbons behind your backs, because I was miserable. I wanted to be something; I wanted so much to be something in your eyes. But now," and she stopped and looked very radiant and at peace as she continued, "for the first time in my life I'm happy to be nothing for Jesus Christ, just to be the mother of our children . . . and Joe's wife."

But almost immediately upon entering this new kind of life Betty had asked us, "What am I going to do about Joe?" This was a question many people had been wondering for years. Joe was a winsome young man in his early thirties who was financially interested in the funeral business in that part of the state. He was also interested in gambling. And to give you an insight into his local reputation at that time, some of his friends called his head funeral parlor, "Joe's Place." We had told Betty to go home and be a different wife, to love Joe and quit trying to change him. Well, the next week Joe showed up at the meeting . . . very suspicious.

One night about sixteen weeks later, Joe led us in a period of de- votion on the cross which was ruggedly beautiful. It was beautiful because it was filtered through a real life which was experiencing sal- vation. And it came to us clearly in our own language without the impediment of religious jargon. When he had finished he said to us, "You know, sixteen weeks ago I came out here to laugh at you, and to prove to Betty that whatever it was she had found I didn't need. But after I'd been here an hour, I knew that this was important. And after two hours I knew you had found what I'd been looking for all my life . . . in all the wrong places. I knew you had found the 'name of the game' . . . the meaning of life."

What we were seeing in this group was God working in the "now," and I cannot describe the sense of joy and elation, the sense of dis- covery and belonging and being loved which almost miraculously developed in these meetings (which paradoxically dealt mainly with the *problems* of giving one's self and one's situation to God and to other people).

As these and later groups continued we found that each time we had to face the danger of becoming an inbred little clique; and we would bring in new people in various ways. But we also began to realize that being a Christian meant more even than the ebb and flow of meeting together in our group on Thursday nights and for worship on Sundays and then going casually out into our separate lives as witnesses. I began to sense that the group was helping some of us to get beyond a vague general approach to our Christian lives in the world. We were beginning to be helped—each to find the particular form or shape of his own obedience away from the group. Two of the older ladies in one group felt impelled to visit the sick and learned to help them in practical ways. Two men were interested in integration and began to get involved in trying to see what they might do that would be both practical and truly Christlike. A doctor and a dentist began to approach their office routine and practices as they might have a foreign mission assignment. And the change in perspective changed both of their lives.

The couple I have called Betty and Joe felt led to change businesses, which entailed breaking lifelong ties and moving to another city at great financial risk. A doctor and his wife in a group in Indiana took a boy, a Cuban refugee, into their home to educate with their daughters while his parents were trapped in Cuba. The wife began visiting a young woman at the county jail and eventually got the woman released to their family's care to help her get a job and back on her feet. Another doctor and his family did the same thing for a nineteen year old boy in Corpus Christi, Texas. These things were not all easy, happy experiences. Yet even with the anguish and uncertainty of the changes and failures we and others were experiencing in these groups, we found a deep and solid joy, a real enjoyment of life in our close association in Christ.

But more important than our immediate enjoyment, we found together that contemporary "Living Christianity" is not what we had thought it was at all. For us it became no longer a religion of sacred patterns of behavior and the study of solemn Reality. We found that it is actually not a "religion" at all, but *real* creative life, life in which we are free to be honest about ourselves and to accept and love each other and Him, because the Living Christ is in the midst of us . . . winning us to Himself and to His world. Suddenly we had something real to tell, something "which we have seen and heard!" Together!

And then I saw my life as a business man from a new perspective . . . and was very disappointed.

Chapter 7

"... no one of us lives, and equally no one of us dies, for himself alone."

(Romans 14:7 NEB)

GOD AND A BUSINESS OFFICE

It has never ceased to amaze me that we Christians have developed a kind of selective vision which allows us to be deeply and sincerely involved in worship and church activities and yet almost totally pagan in the day in, day out guts of our business lives . . . and never realize it. I came to see the appalling extent to which this can be true when after having done four terms of seminary work, served on the vestries of two churches, and taught a large Sunday School class, a man who had worked in the same (oil company) division office I had for over a year said one day, "Gee, Keith, I didn't know you were a Christian." This stunned me into realizing that although I had taken Christ by the hand and led Him through one passage after another in the labyrinth of my soul, I had always left Him at the parking lot when I drove in to go to my office in the major oil company for which I worked.

I prayed about this but couldn't imagine how *I* could witness for Christ in that particular situation. It wasn't that it was so awful. It was just that the language, the risque stories, and the competitive atmosphere left no oxygen for the spoken Gospel to live in. Besides, I had been pretty fast for years with little suggestive innuendoes and an occasional profane outburst. Sigmund Freud has said, very perceptively I think, in his *A General Introduction to Psychoanalysis,* that these unchanged areas in our lives are like nature parks which the city fathers in large metropolitan areas fence off and allow to grow wild just as they always have, so the citizens will have a little piece of the old life to wander through to remember how it used to be.

I think this is what I have done with certain areas in my outward life. Certainly I have done so with areas of my inward thoughts, which I had walled off from the encroachment of the Holy Spirit so that I might leave them just as they always have been. This being the case with me, how was I, of all people, supposed to bring the Living God into my vocational situation?

But I could get no peace in my prayer time until I tried. One morning I arrived at work, went into my private office, and closed the door. I sat down and prayed that God would somehow let me witness for Him that day. Within an hour I had chickened out and was my same old attention-getting self. I was very discouraged.

At this point I stopped. Since I wanted to be Christ's person yet didn't feel that I could effectively (or perhaps safely) do it in this pagan atmosphere, I thought this must be a call to go back to seminary and become a minister. Frankly it would have been simpler in many ways since people *expect* a minister to talk about Christ. But because of family and financial obligations, an investigation seemed to reveal that further education was out of the question. Intensely disappointed I sat in my office one day and consciously surrendered my vocational life to Christ. As I sat there alone, it was as if my eyes were opened for the first time to the situation as it really was. I realized that the stereotype I had carried in my mind all of my life of the Christian minister had blinded me to the fact that God might want me to be His special representative in that office.

But I realized that I really didn't know how to "witness in my vocation." I guess I was afraid it meant getting a basket of tracts as some men do and wandering down the halls making people wish I would get fired so that they wouldn't have to dodge me and my Christian witnessing. This method had never seemed very effective when aimed at me in the past. As a matter of fact now that I was a Christian I hated to be identified with those men (many of whom I knew were fine Christians). It wasn't that what they *said* was wrong; but there seemed to be a cool superiority about their attitude toward us sinners that didn't smack of the love of Christ. I knew that the God who had touched my life had loved me *before* I came to Him, just as I was in all my weakness. There had to be a different way for me.

But there was no trail to follow in this mission field filled with sharp sophisticated young men and women. I did not know even how to begin. To be honest, I was very reticent even to mention Christ's name to most of my associates. After several periods of frustration and procrastination, I decided to take Christ's Presence with me in my conscious mind clear through a day at the office. And this was the beginning. I soon learned that years of contrary thought patterns made it difficult to practice the Presence of Christ between concentrating on business matters. I was convinced that the quality of my work would be an integral part of any Christian witness I might have, so concentration on work was even more necessary. I realized that rather than worry about thinking of Christ all day, a Christian business man must commit a piece of work to God and then really concentrate *on the work.*

To remind myself of God's presence I decided to pray every time I walked to and from the drinking fountain in the hall. Things began to happen. As I walked through the offices and spoke to people, I was praying; and I began to pray for *them.* Although I could not notice any outward difference in my own attitude, some of the love and concern I began to feel for these people must have communicated itself to them, because without my saying anything about my new intention in that situation, people began to come into my private office and talk to me about their inner lives. I soon realized that behind the smooth sophisticated faces in that company were many frustrated, lonely, and often frightened "little boys and girls" reaching out in the darkness of their souls for some meaning, some purpose in life. I began to see the extent of the need for Christ in the lives of "successful" people.

Before long I went to work for another company which was growing at a rapid rate. Another member of the management team there was a concerned Christian, but he, too, was stumped by the problems involved in trying to bring Christ consciously and effectively into a dynamic, hard hitting, and very competitive business situation. We prayed together about it.

One Friday, when the executive vice-president was on a trip around the world and the pressures began to build due to critical business growth, I called my secretary into my office. "Lottie," I said, "I need to pray about this business. Monday morning I am going to come to work a few minutes early and pray in the conference room. If anyone else would like to do this too, they can."

I then went around to the department heads and secretaries and told them the same thing. This sounds very easy as I write it, but it was one of the most difficult things I had ever done in business. That weekend I kicked myself clear around the yard as I mowed it. Now, I had gone too far. It wasn't *my* company; and besides when no one showed up on Monday morning I would lose face as a manager. But I told God I was sorry for my lack of faith, confessed my self-centeredness, and said I was willing to fail for Him . . . I thought.

The next Monday morning almost all of the fourteen people in that office were in the conference room. I realized then that many people really want God to be a part of their vocational lives, but there is no feasible corporate trail to follow. We decided that if God is real enough to be in Christ, there must be an intelligent way to allow Him to become part of the situation of which we were a part. If not, He was too small to be God. We decided to pray for each other and for the people who came into that office, and we asked Christ to come into that company's life through us if it was His will.

This group was made up of people of very diverse religious backgrounds. There were: a Presbyterian, two Roman Catholics, an honest agnostic, several Baptists, an Episcopalian, and one man who was studying Buddhism. We began to know each other on a different level. I began to love some of the ones I had only passed in the halls before. One day the man whom I felt was an agnostic, particularly concerning the person of Christ, came rushing into my office right after lunch and flopped down in a chair, looking very pale. That morning we had been talking about the fact that the Christian life and faith in Christ can only truly be grasped experimentally, through a committing of one's life. This had been hard for this man to see. He had an excellent academic mind. His father was an outstanding professor in biology at a Big Ten University. The young man had received a degree in chemistry and a graduate degree in geology with excellent marks. This idea of the *faith* in Jesus Christ having to come *before* the understanding sounded like intellectual suicide to him.

Now he was sprawled in a chair across from my desk staring at the floor. Finally he looked up and said, "Do you know what just happened to me?"

When I said I didn't, he related this story: It seems that on the way back to the office from lunch he had been driving in a crowded section of the city. Just ahead of him several cars, a young mother had gotten out of a parked automobile and stepped backward right in the path of a truck, which struck her down. It all happened so quickly as he was inching toward the place where the woman's body lay that all he could remember was seeing the look of terror on the three year old little girl's face as she stared down at her mother through the open car door. A policeman had rushed up from the corner and was waving traffic around the accident. As my friend drove by, the dying woman looked up at him sort of pleading . . . and then disappeared from his view as he was motioned ahead in the traffic.

The shock of this incident had made a profound impression on this man opposite me in the chair. It had shattered the shell of intellectual sophistication, he said, inside of which he had been living. It had revealed to him starkly his mortality, and the truth that his real objections to committing his life to Christ were not intellectual at all. They were volitional. He simply didn't like the idea of giving up his will to God or anyone else. And upon realizing this, as he had driven on down the street, he had suddenly known existentially who he was and who God was. In the same moment he wanted deeply to respond to the Christ whose presence and love he now sensed in his own experience. Right there in the car he had consciously committed as much of himself as he could to as much of Christ as he could perceive. He prayed that God would come into his life and reveal Himself more completely.

Needless to say this man's deep conversion, the subsequent newness of life, and sharing with him the thrill of new discovery had a profound effect on several of us. We realized that it had taken place in an atmosphere of love and acceptance over a period of months in the office.

I cannot say that what happened because of our meeting together made the company a lot of money. I cannot even say what the real effect on other people's lives was. I don't know. But the effect in my own was amazing. I saw that it was difficult for a man to swear at one he has just prayed with. I saw that the women in an office have a feeling of being a real part of a living company of people when they have prayed with the men for the direction of their mutually shared vocational life. People began to treat each other more like people. This was true even though everyone was having to work under an unusually heavy burden at that time.

Men began to come in our offices, sit down and say, "What kind of a deal is this—these people laugh as if they were really happy." Together we began to learn to witness, to pray, to communicate what was happening in our lives, to our wives, families and our ministers, learning to adjust to the problems of office situations as *Christian* business men. We had small groups of men coming to our offices to meet once a week to discuss the problems we faced in trying to be God's people in business. We would have sandwiches and discuss the Bible and its authority and relatedness to the new challenges we now saw all around us.

As we struggled with our own problems and those of the Christian business men we knew, we found that it is not easy to take Christ into one's business as Lord. If one is serious, he soon realizes that he must work harder than his non-Christian competitors and do a better job at his business, because he must give up the "leverage" of cutting corners (in the inevitable dishonest practices in business and taxation procedures today). This may cost some money . . . a great deal of money.

People misunderstand your message. We found with Whitehead that, "The success of language in conveying information is vastly overrated especially in learned circles. Not only is language highly elliptical, but also nothing can supply the defect of first hand experience." [1] We came to realize that in the long run in our vocation the only real witness which would last was not what we *said* about our beliefs but what people saw us to *be,* week after week, in our dealings with our associates and our competitors. This was not a glamorous witness, and we made many serious mistakes. We were horrified as we began to see our real

---

1. Alfred North Whitehead, *Adventures of Ideas,* New York: Mentor Books, 1933, p. 286.

business personalities revealed. We were honestly astonished at our continuing selfishness and greed. Often we could only see our failure to witness. But with all of the difficulties, we found that we were experiencing the greatest life we had ever known. We saw the lives of some intelligent, seeking people in our vocational world changing before our eyes. Although we failed in many ways, we found ourselves a part of a Purpose, a Challenge which transcended the oil business.

Gradually we discovered a new sense of freedom from the terrible responsibility to be successful in business *or* in spreading the Gospel. The *outcome,* we realized, was God's business. Ours was to do the 'specifics' before us that day. Life began to be a different experience. We did not need to pressure anyone to accept God's Gift of Himself. The "inner tracking" and actual converting could only be done by Christ. At last I understood what Barth meant when he said about the Message: "I am glad I did not invent it, and hence it is not my responsibility to defend it. My only task and privilege is to tell you that God Himself said so and says so until this day." [2]

We discovered that it was fun (though painful) to try to be honest with one's self. We found that it was appalling to discover the extent to which we deceived ourselves in our vocational lives. We found it crushing to be misunderstood as a Christian. But transcending all these things, there was an inexpressible joy in sharing the experience of a business man as he begins a new life and of watching him begin to live that life for God. But the real revelation I think we found in trying to take Christ with us into our business lives was that the further "out on a limb" we seemed to be going to try to be obedient to Christ's will as we could perceive it, the more *real He* became. This led to the realization that Christ does not promise the business man great material success in his vocation (though this may take place), but rather Christ brings the *inner security* which one seeks through great material success . . . and having found this, the burden of succeeding is lifted. And this inner security is discovered in the day by day relationship with Him.

What might happen to other men or groups of men who try to make their vocations Christian vocations? I do not know; but I think

2. Karl Barth, *Deliverance to the Captives,* Harper and Brothers, 1961.

Dietrich Bonhoeffer came close to the answer when he said, "And if we answer the call to discipleship, where will it lead us? What decisions and partings will it demand? To answer this question we shall have to go to Him, for only He knows the answer. Only Jesus Christ who bids us follow Him, knows the journeys end. But we do know that it will be a road of boundless mercy. Discipleship means joy." [3]

3. Dietrich Bonhoeffer, *The Cost of Discipleship*, New York: The Macmillan Company, 1961, p. 32.

Chapter 8

"*. . . be doers of the word, and not hearers only, deceiving yourselves.*"

(James 1:22 RSV)

SHARING THE NEW WINE

As I began seriously to try to discover a way to articulate something of the reality I was finding in my own experience, I realized almost immediately that "saying words" is not what is meant by communicating the Reality of Jesus Christ. I think this is true regardless of how theologically correct the words may be.

In my reaction against legalistic, verbal religious "scalp gathering," I had for years decided that I would *live* my faith instead of *talk* about it. Now, I saw how totally selfish this "live the faith and not talk about it" idea is. It reminds me of a man in a dread disease ward marvelously meeting the doctor who had perfected a cure. The patient, as he was being (secretly) cured, walked back and forth in the same ward sort of flexing his muscles as he moved beds around and variously helped the other patients *die more comfortably*. His display of new wholeness only led the other patients to envy *him* . . . leaving their own deep illness unattended to. I saw that this patient had to somehow *introduce his dying fellows to the physician* so that they too could begin to be healed from their loneliness and incompleteness. I realized that I was this patient. This introduction to Christ, I saw, would take some *words* of direction or at least indication.

As I began to ask outstanding Church leaders how one person might tell another about the realness of God, I found that this business of effectively communicating Christian Reality, of "witnessing," is probably one of the least understood areas of Christian living today, particularly among educated people. Everyone I went to beat around the bush. They simply did not know how to do this without being pious or obscure. I decided to try to see for myself what true effectiveness in sharing the Christian message and life might include. Immediately I was stumped.

Who can properly judge his own true effectiveness in other people's lives? For years, when things went wrong around our house I would try to "make things right" by bringing Mary Allen a present. But even if the surprise were a good one, it never seemed to strike a really deep chord of response. I sensed that she was somehow disappointed, though she managed to hide it well.

On the other hand I can remember a particularly cold and snowy winter night in Indiana. It was after supper. The wind was howling outside and we felt very cozy. Mary Allen was doing some sewing in one corner, and I was trying to read the newspaper on the sofa across the room. Our three little girls were giggling and climbing all over me as if I were a ladder. Finally I stopped trying to read and began to wrestle with them and love them. Through the tangle of little arms and legs I happened to see Mary Allen across the room . . . with tears of happiness streaming down her face.

I began to see that I, and the people I know, are most winsome in all our intimate relationships when we are unconsciously *being ourselves* with other people and accepting them just as they are, *without trying to manipulate or change them in any way.* But the very lack of self-consciousness that is so attractive makes those things we do at such times most difficult to analyze.

A minister often thinks he is most effective for God in the pulpit on that Sunday morning when he is preaching an eloquent sermon after hours of preparation. But between the nine and eleven o'clock services when he is in the process of going from one service to another—trying to relax a moment—someone urgently grabs his arm and says, "The superintendent of the children's department didn't come this morning!" So the minister has to go into the children's chapel and speak. He goes in and shares informally something of himself or the Gospel message, never knowing as he rushes out to the next service that the mind of a little visitor on the back row was struck by his impromptu words . . . and offered itself to God. Perhaps a great Christian life has been conceived . . . and the minister never knows.

I think a great deal of what happens deeply and positively to other people through our lives happens in this way. But, on the other hand, I found that there are a great many things we *can* learn consciously about sharing the newness of the Christian Life and Message. Most committed Christians have a great deal they could say about the reality and love of God, the relief of forgiveness, and the gift of purpose and relatedness to a life once filled with confusion and lack of meaning. Most of us have some things we might share in our business and social lives if only we knew how to go about it with real perception in the language we use for everyday living, so that we won't be hypocritical. The new groups of lay disciples in America are finding that one can sometimes get this message of salvation and a new life across. I want to discuss here specifically one way this can be done, or attempted, in the lives of people like many of us in the church today.

First of all I think there are at least three levels of communicating Living Christianity; and most of the people with whom I had been acquainted only knew about the first level. For the great majority of church going people effective sharing of Christianity consists of studying the Bible and related books, speaking to lay groups about God, Sunday School teaching, preaching, living the Christian ethical life, being a good churchman, husband, and business man, having an active concern for the important social and political issues of our time, and helping the poor. Most of us think a man who does all these things (layman or minister) is really getting God's message across. Often such a person develops quite a reputation as a speaker and Christian leader. But as important as this level of Christian sharing is, I have become convinced that it is only "contact work" for the Lord; and for years we have made it the whole enterprise. This type of Christian living and speaking often spreads a warm religious aura in a group; but it leaves few deeply and permanently changed lives in its wake. And without deeply changed and growing lives, there can be no "Renewed Church," no changed world, regardless of how full the churches are.

The second level of Christian sharing is that which is being reborn in the life of the church today. It is a person to person ministry, an actual conscious readiness on the part of an individual Christian to put another man or woman in touch with the Living God. This is not another "pat system" or "semi-canned sales pitch." It is rather a way of thinking about and being related to other people. It is an attitude based on the realization that behind the remarkably placid masks of the faces we see every day on the streets and in our businesses and clubs there lies a world of twisting souls, living with frustration and the fear of failure and meaninglessness, a world of souls without rudders, without any real sense of ultimate direction.

As I have implied earlier I think we in America may be the "masters of deceit" in our personal lives. We have even deceived ourselves. We wear masks of success and happiness and integrity so much that we have even convinced ourselves that we are not such a bad people. Consequently we have not the basic prerequisite for coming to God . . . a conscious sense of sin or separation from Him. Or at least so it would appear. Modern writers have made much of the lack of man's sense of sin today. Reinhold Niebuhr speaks of "the universality of this easy conscience among moderns."[1] Although I think this generalization is far too broad, I do know that many people in our generation do not sense their basic separation from God (or Sin) as *guilt*. Today this separation often manifests itself in the vague indefinable restlessness and incompleteness we have been discussing. So if one goes about trying to capitalize on men's conscious guilt to get them into a personal relation with God, he may miss many of the sharpest people all together and drive them away from Christ, since they simply don't experience their basic problem as guilt.

I have spoken to dozens of groups of all sizes and hundreds of individuals these past few years; and I have never faced a group in which I was not convinced that many of the people were crying out in the privacy of their own hearts for some peace and direction in their souls. What I am saying is that there is a *very real need* for the life and message Christ brings; and this need is not far beneath the surface of modern life. This needs to be said since so many people are dis-

---

1. Reinhold Niebuhr, *The Nature and Destiny of Man*, New York: Charles Scribner's Sons, 1941, Vol. 1, p. 94. See also D. M. Baillie, *God Was in Christ*, New York, Charles Scribner's Sons, p. 162f. for Baillie's view on modern man's lack of a sense of sin.

couraged about sharing the Christian life when people look so self-sufficient all around them.

This is the way this kind of sharing might work. First, you find yourself in contact with another person, a natural, normal contact. Right here I think many Christians get off the track. I am so egotistical that when I became a Christian I was sure that I was sent to witness to the most outstanding group I knew (whom I considered my peers). But in reading the New Testament I was somewhat stunned to realize that even Jesus Christ evidently never made it in His own home town, with his own local peer group. (Mark 6:1 f.) And this did not seem to disturb nor deter Him in the least.

So I began to look around me at all the people whom God had already put in my life with whom I might develop a deeper and more personal relationship. I realized that without changing my daily routine one bit, I had a world filled with people, most of whom I had for years been ignoring. There was the man who sometimes helped me in the yard. There were the fellows in the gas station I traded with all the time, the Negro parking lot attendants, the service people in the office building my office was in, the waiters at the Petroleum Club, the secretaries, the bank tellers, and other men with whom I had coffee occasionally . . . and my own wife and children. As I began to see these people as *important people* who need God and His love, I realized that many of us active American Churchmen are stumbling over the bodies of our wives and children and people in our daily paths to get out in the time-consuming promoted evangelistic programs to find someone to love for Jesus Christ.

As I began to read the New Testament accounts I saw that Christ almost never "went out of His way" to help anyone. He seems to have walked along and helped the people in His path. He was totally focused on doing God's will and going where God led Him. *But* He never failed to help the people He met along the way while going where God directed Him. This made for an amazing steadiness and spiritual economy in His direction and ministry. This one change in my perspective made witnessing not a program but a *way of life.*

The second thing I realized was that we Christians have so cheapened the Christian message that most thinking people don't want any part of it. Our attitude betrays our lack of real faith. We act as if we were selling tickets to something, or memberships, instead of introducing people to Almighty God in an eternal and conscious relationship. When a person buys a theater ticket he doesn't even have to think about it, it is such a casual thing; and his attitude and verbal exchange with the ticket girl reflects this. But when you walk into a room in which two large corporations are about to consummate a merger, there is an air of gravity. Even a casual observer can tell that something important is taking place—because of the attitudes of the participants as they go about their business.

I think non-Christians do not read this kind of importance into our attitude when we are talking to them about Christianity. So I would say that in this kind of witnessing, we must think and pray in terms of a much larger God, a much greater and more transforming Gift of Life. I came to see that if people do not really believe we have found something that is terribly important to us, why should they want it?

After an outward personal contact has been made, then the *real* contact is made with the person behind the mask. I have found that this is done mostly by *listening* with real interest. What you are doing when you are listening as a Christian is putting your hand quietly in the other man's life and feeling gently along the rim of his soul until you come to a crack, some frustration, some problem or anguish you sense that he may or may not be totally conscious of. As you are listening, you are loving this person and accepting him just as he is. The magic of this kind of concern is that you will often find your conversation moving imperceptibly from the general surface talk of the world situation and the weather into the intimate world of families and of hopes, of his life and yours. This change of climate sometimes takes place in a very short time in a listening atmosphere of concern and trust.

Everyone today seems to be inwardly yearning for someone who really cares enough just to listen to him, without trying to change him. We don't even listen to each other this way in our own families very often. I am convinced that this fact is one of the key reasons for the tremendous amount of marital infidelity in this country. I do not believe that American men are possessed with an unnaturally strong sex drive. But having a mistress, for instance, is having one who really knows a man's weakness and listens to him and accepts him anyway, just as he is.

But when one begins to listen honestly to people for Christ's sake with a word or look of encouragement, they often begin to cast out before you the shadows of a great number of the fears and uncertainties which are crouching just inside their hearts. Of course this account is greatly oversimplified for some relationships, but not for many (if you are really interested in the person).

In approaching life this way, do *not* think of the person you are listening to as a prospect for the church or as an object for your Christian witness. I know this may sound strange, but if you do think in these terms this will become a kind of spiritual manipulation. And instead of really listening you will be saying to yourself, "How can I get this conversation around to *spiritual* things." Besides, from the other person's perspective your anxiety to get your "Christian content" across sends out the unspoken message that you have something more important on your mind (he doesn't know what it is) than him and what he has to say.

So I began to merely listen to people with the idea in mind of making friends for Christ. Soon I found that I could identify with almost every problem or sin I heard—if not with the deed, certainly with the emotion behind it. And this honest identification freed people to be their real selves. It became a bridge across which we could walk into each other's real lives. I found my life filled with a new and deeper kind of friendship than I had ever known before. But the point is that this kind of sharing begins not by spouting your *answer,* but by finding out who this person is and his problem, his need . . . *as he sees it.*

In the Gospels I do not see Christ rushing up to people, grabbing them by the arm, and confronting them with a theological question. He seems to have walked down the road and listened to people describe their problems as they saw them. The people seemed to be so surprised and thrilled that someone saw their problems and took them seriously, that I rather imagine many responded totally and were made whole. And yet Christ knew these men's basic problem was not withered hands or leprosy. But He met them where they were.

If and when your friendship with someone grows (and it so often will if you love him), and he acknowledges sometime that his life is not complete, *then* very naturally and simply you may want to tell him how you came to a realization in your own life that it wasn't what it should be and how that realization caused you to turn to God. Tell your friend what God did, not to make you *good* (Christ was pretty clear about his attitude toward men claiming goodness. See Mark 10:18) but to make you *basically more joyful.* And if you are not basically more joyful *regardless of the many new problems you have as a Christian,* then you had better take a close look at your own relationship with Christ. You may have missed something very important in the Gospel yourself.

When you have reached this point you will know whether or not this person is cooly detached or obviously seeking something in his own life. You know this because you have listened to him over a period of time and know his real interests and needs. But if after hearing about your life, he says something like, "Yes, uh . . . uh . . . say did you hear what the Yankees did yesterday?" don't panic, feel rejected, and say urgently, "What did I say to offend you?" or, "Don't you understand, Friend, I'm about to lead you to salvation." But rather you might say something more like, "No, what did the Yankees do?" and listen to him. He may only be backing off because you are getting too close to him.

People are spiritually like fawns, ready to dart away at the first sign of what they consider any invasion of privacy. And since you are *not* selling anything, you do not have to be anxious. We Christians are the only people around who claim to have an eternal life; and yet in our urgency to *convince* people, we reflect nothing but anxiety and tenseness. But if this person has listened to your telling something about your own life and relationship to God and is interested, then you must, I believe, help him to see where *he* is now with regard to the gift of new life God is waiting to give him.

This is one way you can help him find out where he is in his relationship to Christ. Get him to look inside his own life, honestly. He doesn't have to tell you what he sees (this allows him to keep his privacy while considering what you are saying). Ask him to be specific with himself and with God. Let's say, so that you can see how it might feel to be talked to like this, that you and I are sitting across a luncheon table in a quiet place. We have known each other for some months and have come to the place in our relationship which I have just described. You have been a churchman for years, but you are not experiencing the kind of newness in your adult Christian life which we have been discussing. You are really interested in knowing how you might make a new beginning in your own life. I will talk to you here as I would if we were together in the same room. If you are interested, then do the things I will ask you to do.

The first thing I would like for you to do is to look into your own inner life and ask yourself the question, "What is the most important thing in the world to me?" The temptation is to say, "God," but let me tell you some ways you can tell what is really most important to you. What do you think about again and again when your mind is not engaged with work or with someone else? Let me give you some suggestions of the kinds of things I mean: Do you think about your wife or husband (or children)? Do you think about being great in your vocation? Or being considered a brilliant person? Or socially sophisticated? Or are your recurring thoughts about sex or your own beauty? Or are your thoughts when alone centered in your own problems, jealousy etc. . . . centered in yourself? When I ask myself this, some of the things I have come up with at various times in my life (if I am honest) are: Thinking about myself as a successful athlete, business man, scholar, or writer. Or thinking about sexual conquests. Or imagining or hoping people will think I am an extremely intelligent person. Or at one time my thoughts were occupied with how I could become a great Christian minister.

Now each of these thoughts is like a rubber ball on a string tied to the center of your mind. You throw it out and get busy with the work of the day. But when you are alone, back it comes again and again to sit in the middle of the stage of your attention. I am asking you to consider this because whatever you focus this hottest intensity of your mind on is very likely *what you worship instead of Jesus Christ!* For what is worship if it is not the object of your life's most intense focus?

I am not implying that Christ says that it is wrong to love one's children or wife or vocation. But it is wrong to love them more than God. It is wrong to make idols of them. It ruins them and us. I believe that Christ intimates that we can never fully realize the gift of Life which He came to bring us until we first know that we have loved ourselves and our way more than Him and His way (Matt. 9:10-13; Luke 15 and 18:18-30 etc.).

I have become convinced that the things which keep us from a live relationship to Christ are often not the "bad" things in our lives, but the good things which capture our imaginations and keep them from focusing on Jesus Christ.[2] I think this accounts for a good bit of our frustration as churchmen. We look around in our lives and say, "No stealing, no murder, no adultery! Why, God, am I so miserable and frustrated in my Christian life?" But we have not seen the fact that we have never really offered Him the one thing He requires—our primary love.

What does one do when he finds out that he loves something more than God? For me it was rather terrifying, because the thing which was keeping me from the freedom of Christ was *my desire to be a great minister!* Because one's decisions will ultimately be made to conform with the shape of whatever has truly captured his imagination, my own decisions and sacrifices were not being made purely to love and feed Christ's sheep out of obedience and love of Him; but rather my decisions were made to help "the church's work" (*my* work) to its greatest fulfillment. This led to chaos and frustration.

When one sees, and can honestly face the fact, that his world is really centered in something besides God, in one's self in fact, I think he faces the most profound crossroads in his life (whether he is a layman or a Bishop). Because this is to recognize that one has separated himself from God by taking God's place in the center of his own little world.

What does a person do? The answer is paradoxically the simplest and yet the most difficult thing I have ever done. In our age of complexity we want a complex answer, but Christ gives us instead a terribly

---

2. See discussion of this point in William Law's *A Serious Call to a Devout and Holy Life*, Philadelphia: The Westminister Press, 1955, Chapter VII.

difficult one. I think there are basically two things involved in coming to God at the center of one's life: (1) To tell God that we do *not* love Him most, and confess specifically what it is that we can not give up to Him. (2) To ask God in the personality of Jesus Christ to come into our conscious lives through His spirit and show us how to live our lives for Him and His purposes . . . one day at a time.[3]

But what if you recognize that you *honestly do not* want God more than whatever is first in your life? I think this is where a good many perceptive Christians find themselves. In that case I would recommend that you (1) Confess (as above) and then (2) tell Christ that your honest condition is that you cannot even *want* Him most. But tell Him that you *want to want* Him most (if you do), ask Him to come into your life at a deeper level than you have ever let Him before, and give Him permission to win you totally to Himself. This may be your first honest encounter with Christ, and He will take you wherever you are. As a matter of fact I believe this is really all *any* of us can do . . . give God *permission* to make us His. We certainly cannot be His by our own strength of will.

And if you made this new conscious beginning in a conversation with me, this is what I would tell you: that from now on you are not responsible to exert the pressure, the burden of muscling yourself up to be "righteous." You are not *promising* to change, or to *have strength,* or to be a *great* Christian. You have only confessed your need and turned your life over to Christ. What a relief! If He wants me to

---

3. I am aware of the arguments of Buber and others against the position that: Once a man recognizes his idol as such, he can immediately turn the same kind of love on God. The Buber position points out (correctly, I think) that the love of idols is a possessive love, and that if we turn this same kind of love on God, we will blaspheme: "He who has been converted by this substitution of object now 'holds' a phantom that he calls God. But God, the eternal Presence, does not permit Himself to be *held.* Woe to the man so possessed that he thinks he possesses God." (*I and Thou* p. 106)

Since I believe that kind of substitution of one's possessive love has led many Evangelical Christians into a state of frustrated misery, I have here been careful to explain that the change I am referring to is from the possessive love of an idol to the *responding* love which is directed to the One we want to *possess us,* to guide us, to confront us at the core of our being with *His* Lordship and Life.

change, He will furnish the motivating power by giving me the desire to change, and then the strength to do it.[4]

But how does one begin living this new life every day? If a man makes this sort of new beginning in your presence, don't clap him on the back and walk off whistling. This is a terrifying experience to decide suddenly to give God your will, only to realize that you don't know what to do next. Christianity is not a *status* at which one arrives; it is a *life* in which one matures. So show him the first steps one begins to take in this life with God.

Show him how to take a few minutes a day, *each* day, to begin developing this new relationship. Tell him how to begin reading the Bible every day, and to begin to live and move into it. Tell him to look for the personality of God in all that he does and sees. Show him how to get started at once in a vital sharing life with other strugglers. Take him into your own group and admit you are a struggler too. And if you don't have such a group in your own church, look for one or start one for your own sake. Explain to this person the discouragements that will come in actually trying to live your life for God; describe the doubts; and point beyond them to the joys. Be honest, because there *are* doubts and discouragements; and unless he knows that *you* have them, he may doubt his own faith as they hit him when he is all alone.

This kind of sharing of the Christian life and Gospel produces more than attenders at church (though it always should produce these). For people who have seen themselves and accepted Christ as Lord and Master of their practical lives have not crossed the finish line of the Christian life; for the first time they have climbed down out of the grandstand and gotten on the starting block as participants in that life in the *Living Body of Christ*.

So, as the first level of sharing Christianity is talking on Christian

---

4. This is not advising Christians to sit back and do nothing. It is rather a statement of the paradoxical fact that although good works are *inevitable* in the deeply committed Christian's life, I do not believe they are *required* to *establish* or *maintain* one's redeemed relationship. The relationship and the strength to live the life are gifts of Grace.

subjects, Church School teaching and Christian living, this second person to person level is the far more demanding business of living life, consciously loving person after person, listening to each one personally, privately, and then walking a few steps with him toward the cross, and perhaps putting his hand quietly into the waiting hand of Christ . . . and His Church.

Chapter **9**

". . . *you put new wine into fresh skins; then both are preserved.*"

(Matthew 9:17 NEB)

WHAT ABOUT THE
OLD WINESKINS

What happens to a man or woman in modern American church life who suddenly finds a completely new orientation by making a serious beginning commitment to find and follow God's will? Paradoxically many of us have found this sense of newness and deep engagement with life contrary to all our honest expectations as conscientious church attenders.

I remember one person with whom I prayed about such a new life several years ago. She had not been well for some time. When she opened her life deeply to God, she found that she could accept herself and her situation for the first time in years. Within a week she was off the sedation she had been told would be a part of her life from then on. She was radiant to see as she began struggling to learn to live with Christ in the center of things. I suggested that she tell her minister. She had been a loyal churchgoer for years; and it was natural to want to share her new discovery with her pastor. She went to him joyously. But his reaction was not one of joy. It was a grim and frowning response. She was urged not to get excited and be emotional. This would wear off and she should not do anything foolish. She was crushed. And if she had not had a small fellowship of people who accepted and loved her and allowed her to be freely joyful about God, she might have despaired and not found the tremendous and mature joy she subsequently has discovered.

Why did the minister react this way? This is not an isolated incident. This same scene has been repeated to my personal knowledge

dozens of times during these past years. This growing body of new
Christian disciples is constantly amazed at certain ministers' (often in
their own denominations) rejection of them. This question must be
faced if the new life being experienced by God's people is to be chan-
neled through the existing structures of the institutional church.

So let's look at this problem briefly. First, from the *minister's* perspective what would an encounter like the one just described with
one of his faithful parishioners look like? This minister had received
his theological education at a large and academically respectable Divinity School. He had been a professional minister for almost twenty
years, a member of several important regional denominational committees (chairman of one), and had seen his parish grow in number
of communicants and in size of financial budget rather substantially
in the years since the war. This man would be classified as a successful
Christian minister.

But now this woman comes to see him who has been faithfully listening to his sermons for years. She says that all these years she has missed
the boat spiritually (under him). She implies (he thinks) that he
didn't really tell her about Jesus Christ. Fortunately (he hears her to
say), she has at last found the *real* truth of the Gospel message; and
finding the truth she has committed her life to Christ.

"How did you find out?" the minister asks.

"Why through a friend, a layman."

"What is this layman's theological background?"

"Well, he has been in the oil exploration business for ten years.
And he is a Christian."

In any case, she has found a new and joyous experience of life and
wanted to share it with him. All this is fantastic to the minister who
has been preaching about the atonement and redemption for years.
Her account sounds to a trained theological mind like the rankest kind
of oversimplification . . . almost sawdust trail. He immediately suspects
that this dear woman has been duped by some fanatic, and he is trying
to think of some way to politely squelch all this before she gets badly
hurt. He went through three years of tough postgraduate study,
preached and exhorted for years, and now one of his key people comes
to him spewing what sounds like nineteenth century piety and implying

(from *his* perspective) that *he* has missed the boat altogether. Not only that, but she is claiming to have found a kind of joy and new insight into her own life and into the meaning of the Gospel which he knows is bound to be unreal . . . because he has never experienced it himself. And certainly he has sincerely wanted and prayed for whatever God has to offer man.

But let's look at the same encounter from the point of view of the renewed Christian. After years of searching she has found in the past few weeks in her soul the meaning of life. God's forgiving love has suddenly become *real* to her. She loves Christ and His sinful people and realizes that she is truly one of them and is grossly self-centered. But she sees at the same time that she has been accepted and does not have to be the pious Pharisee any more. She has only to be loving and obedient to Christ's will as she can determine it, day by day. The burden of having to be a social leader is gone; and she can be herself at long last. She can adjust her priorities, take care of her family, and help other people for Christ's sake. She has begun to become involved in doing this individually, through the church, and through social agencies aligned with her Lord's purposes. She has validated her experience in the pages of the New Testament (which before had seemed grossly exaggerated) and in the living contemporary experiences of a small group of people meeting weekly to find out who they really are and what Christ and His purposes mean in our time.

So she goes to tell her minister about what is happening to her, which she is sure he has been praying for for years. But he is cold and, of all things, (from her perspective) he rejects her personally. She is trying to tell him that she has seen her self-rightous behavior as a churchwoman, and at last has begun to understand Christian love in a small group of friends she meets with on Tuesday nights. But the minister only looks at her with a poorly disguised pained and almost patronizing look (again from *her* perspective) and tries to imply that all she has found is illusory and will soon depart.

Now as this woman's experience deepened over the next months and years (instead of disappearing) her relationship with her minister and her confidence in him became increasingly difficult to maintain. So she began to pray with her little group that *her minister would change and find the light.* And had he heard that he was being prayed for in this way he would have been furious. We would have had two people confronting each other (or even two factions, since the little group had grown) each thinking the other had missed the point, each praying to the same Lord that the other would change to his vision of what a Christian is. And then the church organizational life and the pulpit would have become battle grounds for getting the respective points of view across. Everyone would be hurt and frustrated and deeply threatened. And agape love would tiptoe quietly out the window.

Finally in some cases, in desperation at this growing and uncontrollable "menace," some ministers have rallied their denominational leaders and tried to build a dam across the channel of this stream of "fanaticism" in the church.

What can be done to prevent this sequence of misunderstandings and painful encounters which can be multiplied by continually larger numbers every year? In the first place the lady parishioner could have gone to her minister and thanked him for his patience and prayers over the past ten years. And (if she had known how) she might have used his language by telling him that she was beginning to become aware of the totality of God's call upon one's priorities, and that she wanted now to begin to study the faith which was at last becoming existentially real for her. But she had no way to know how to do this in his language.

Or the minister might have listened with real interest and joy at one of his flock's new discovery of the Gospel message, and then suggested that the two of them stop and give thanks in prayer together for this wonderful new beginning. He could have realized that newly-committed lay men and women are not supposed to articulate like C. S. Lewis or William Stringfellow. He could have tried to understand that they are filled only with love and a sense of release. He could have seen that most laymen do not have philosophically trained minds; and that when he rejected the *terms* of this woman's theological statement that she could not separate her statement from herself, and only felt his *personal* rejection.

One of the causes for this kind of conflict is, in my opinion, a misunderstanding of the practical sequence of consequences which may follow genuine conversion. When any human love relationship becomes deeply personal, and real commitment ensues, there is a period of adjusting to the centering of one's attention and concern from self to another. For some reason this transition always seems to include an almost exclusive preoccupation with the beloved. The best human analogy might be the honeymoon period in marriage. All the happy bride can talk about is "my George." She is convinced that their relationship will somehow miraculously by-pass the otherwise universal problems of marriage. And during this period of rose colored living she is virtually oblivious of other responsibilities and people. Her elders in the pilgrimage of marriage can only smile and help her adjust to the shocks and surprises as they come and wait for her to pass through to a mature relationship to the world.

In the deep kind of personal Christian commitment the New Testament calls for, a similar phenomenon often seems to take place. All the new Christian can talk about is "Jesus and me." The new love and devotion to his Lord often makes the starry-eyed Christian seem to his minister selfish and oblivious of his social and institutional duties. And for all practical purposes he may not be worth shooting for six months with regard to meaningful articulation or burden bearing in the church's program. Paul may have spent several years in this period (Galatians 1:17); Augustine spent months.[1] And during this honeymoon period the new Christian needs encouragement, patience, and help in trying to learn to live in his new Christ-centered life. When he does not receive these things, he is not likely to go to his minister to find the direction toward maturity as he comes out of the honeymoon and begins to look for the shape of his particular obedience in the world.

I think that another of the primary causes for the language and communication barriers between committed laymen and their ordained ministers stems from mistaken ideas about "commitment" and the "ministry." When I was first in the oil business and had become aware

---

1. *The Confessions of St. Augustine*, New York: E. P. Dutton and Company, Inc., 1951, See Book IX, p. 189f.

that I wanted to know God as He is revealed in Jesus Christ, I started to read books and ask questions about the faith. I began to teach an occasional Sunday School class and became active in the church's program. Before long people would say, "You ought to be a minister." The implication was that if a layman's commitment and involvement rise to a certain level, he will love Christ enough to go to seminary and become an ordained pastor. Ordination, therefore, in the eyes of the average layman has become a religious status symbol of total commitment. And some are afraid to make a serious commitment, since they know they are not cut out to be ordained ministers.

I remember that I went to seminary because I wanted to serve God in the fullest way possible—even though I honestly *did not* want to become a parish minister, nor did I feel called to be. But unknowingly the church has sometimes implied that if you are *really serious* about wanting to serve God totally, this decision is tantamount to a call to the ordained ministry. But I do *not* believe this is true—nor scriptural. In the earliest New Testament accounts, committed Christians within the fellowship were set aside or ordained for certain special tasks or *functions*. The first deacons were appointed and set apart by the laying on of hands to wait tables (Acts 6:1-6). These men were ordained not because they had reached a certain level of commitment which other Christians had not reached; but they were ordained because someone trustworthy was needed to *wait on the tables.*

I believe this is still true in the Christian community—that men are ordained to preach (for example) not because they are the most committed, but because they have been given certain specialized gifts to be used to help equip God's (equally committed) people for work in His service "to the building up of the body of Christ," the whole Church (See Ephesians 4:11f). But as long as an ordained pastor feels (even unconsciously) that his decision to become ordained and his subsequently acquired theological education are signs of a will *more* given to God than that of a committed lawyer or housewife, then that pastor will think of his language as the true language of commitment. He will try to educate his people to become as he is, a trained theologian—instead of helping them to become the *creative business men and parents and housewives* they were born to be. In short, as an

equipping minister he will teach them to use their own language for
Christ's sake rather than try to make them learn his systematic specialized language before he will accept them as being truly committed.

I believe a good many of the misunderstandings between the renewed
Christians in our generation and their ordained ministers center around
these different views of commitment and ministry, however unconsciously they may be held. But even to solve the thousands of unpleasant personal encounters would not get at the heart of the basic problem here. The question is: can this new wine *ever* be poured into the
old wineskins without bursting them?

The option lies with the Institutional Church. The nature of the
new life being breathed into the Church today is historically such that
it cannot be denied a chance to express itself. Its main stream is based
solidly on a scriptural, historical revelation of the mighty acts of God
in Christ. These new people are experiencing God's Living Presence
together in the contemporaneity of His Holy Spirit. Above all, these
new disciples are mediating carriers of Christ's redeeming love to His
world. The building stones of the Protestant Churches are held together by mortar made from the blood of such people. Unfortunately
it seems that they are only recognizable in the flowing robes of the
past.

I do not agree with those who have "given up" on the Institutional
Church, as difficult as the situation sometimes seems to be to ministers
and laymen. I think there *is* a way. The new wine will not burst the
old wineskins *if* the handlers of the old wineskins will receive the new
wine and pour it quickly into new skins themselves. This is already
happening in many places. And where it is, churches are coming alive
with new and deeper involvement with God in His contemporary redeeming activity. Men and women are being reborn to new purpose
and loyalty in Christ's love. Such churches are becoming centers for
small groups of struggling Christians to come together for worship and
training. Many are finding totally new meaning in the Sacraments and
the Word. Many times such parishes find that their people have come
across denominational lines to learn to be God's priesthood of gentle-
warriors, moving out creatively into the social and moral complexities
of our generation.

What goes on in such a parish? What do the new wineskins look like? They are taking many different shapes; but they all seem to have one thing in common: they all call for a kind of dying of our ecclesiastical ego—for those of us who are ministers professionally. We who have been trained to be the central actor in the liturgical drama, played out in the center of the parish stage, have long had our people as the paying audience. God has been in the wings whispering the minister's cues. But now the minister is being called on to become the backstage prompter in the wings while his *lay people* play out the drama of contemporary redemption on the larger stage of their homes and communities and the world . . . with God, the author of the drama, as the audience!

This means a drastic rethinking of the term ministry (which has been and is being undertaken all around us in the church). The idea of the equipping minister (see Ephesians 4) is becoming a reality in the parishes mentioned above. Pastors are counseling with small struggling groups and individuals about how to study, where to locate resource people, how to find the particular shape of their own obedience in specific moral, ethical and social situations in their vocational worlds. The pastors are having to realize that God did not call His people to be a nation of academically proficient theological or critical Biblical exegetes. They are realizing that at the grass roots level God is not in the academic theologian producing business. He is in the *life changing* business![1] And to change men's lives in relationship to Himself and to each other, God must be in intimate touch with those who do not know of Him and His love.

Since the professional parish minister today is often not in intimate touch with pagan man where he lives and works, the new missionary and minister of Christ to this generation's vocational, social, and political life must be the *Christian layman*. This means that the parish minister must love Christ enough to die to the centrality of his role in

---

1. This line of thinking is not anti-intellectual nor anti-doctrine. I believe a deeply committed Christian will inevitably study and learn all he can propositionally about his faith. But I am convinced that the *focus* of his life must be on living in relationship with God and His people, rather than on the acquisition of knowledge about these things.

the church. He must become the coach, the teacher and pastor of the laymen who will be the new focus of attention in the developing renewal movement. He must in a real sense love Christ more than his own life.

For years people have been saying things like this from the pulpit and the press, but the parish minister has cynically known from bitter experience that laymen simply have neither been willing nor able to articulate the faith as effective missionaries. But that is just the point. *They are beginning to now!* The problem is that many ministers who have prayed and preached for this are afraid to trust the laymen with the Message for fear that they will somehow misrepresent and oversimplify it. Of *course* we will contaminate the Gospel (As *everyone* does. Certainly as between Barth *or* Tillich, one must be contaminating it). But God does not primarily need precise orators, he needs Channels, Lovers! Certainly Christ Himself and Paul *et al* did not fear to trust this message to the theologically untrained people whose lives had been made new by it. Nor in the long run can we.

But what then is the committed Christian's job as a minister (ordained or unordained)? I believe the new wine calls for a revolutionary kind of ministry more profound and exciting than at any time in the past for both laymen and pastors. The layman must not only share his life and Christ's concerned love in the most complex age in history, but he must learn to help God *reproduce reproducers* for His ministry in the world. This is the third and most penetrating level of sharing Christianity.

This kind of Christian ministry consists of getting together with one or two or twelve men who have already begun to give their wills to God and who are hungry to know Him and His will for their lives. One way to begin is to start meeting at least weekly and spending the time it takes over the weeks and months and years to pour your whole cup into theirs. You share together with the utmost honesty the current problems *you* are having as an individual and as a minister in trying to be wholly Christ's person. You learn to study together the scriptures (and later devotional classics and perhaps history and theology along with the Bible) relating your study constantly to your personal lives and the practical ways in which the message may be lived out in your own homes and communities. You teach people to lead and teach other people individually or in other small groups. You pray for each other and other people specifically. You let your life and your concern win you the right to be heard by the church as well as the pagan world. And you, as leader, hold back nothing in your teaching and life.

This seems at first glance the illogical way. Only the greatest ministers have had the perception to overcome the temptation to spend all their time with larger groups. But historically, real spiritual leadership seems to have been passed from man to man individually. Certainly Biblical history indicates this. Moses was told to find a man; and Joshua led the people of the next generation in the actual conquering Moses had dreamed of. Elijahs have chosen their Elishas and God has continued to have other mouthpieces in succeeding generations. And in the New Testament, look at the way Paul operated: he always had one or two with him, pouring himself into them, and teaching them to pour themselves into a few others—Timothy, Titus, Aristarchus, Mark—a few in each place, on each journey, into whom he was quietly building the vision of his soul and demonstrating to them how it could be given to others.

In the Galilean life of Christ this principle of ministry is supremely demonstrated. Jesus evidently spent about two-thirds of His active ministry with *twelve men*. And He did not give the twelve a formal education. As Bishop Newbigin has put it, he did not give these twelve a systematized course. "Being with Him they received not so much a formal course of instruction in divine truth as an introduction into the intimacy of His Spirit"[2] . . . of His life with God. Through these twelve and Paul and his disciples, a multiple progression of life changing lives began.

Historians are often amazed that a handful of virtually uneducated men by the world's standards, with no social or political connections of importance—no program—no systematic theology or plan—no budget—no mass media (or even the corpus of the New Testament for several hundred years)—could begin transforming a large part of the whole world's concept of the character and purposes of God for

2. Lesslie Newbigin, *The Household of God*, New York; Friendship Press, 1960, p. 62.

men. It is particularly baffling that this one sect burst forth from the empty tomb and began covering the earth. Even acknowledging the tremendously propitious time in history which Christ came, the development of Christianity is amazing.

But the world did not see Paul on those lonely nights in the wilds of Tarsus mountains, or in Macedonia, or at Ephesus, often tired from working all day as we do (To call Paul a "layman" may be considered specious thinking, but he was in the transient home building business and seemed to consider his lay vocational status an important aspect of his witness—I Corinthians Chapter 9), pouring his life with Christ carefully into the souls of Silas and Timothy. Paul was not just preaching a message; he was loving and training the children of a family which was to inherit the earth.

But this kind of ministry is so threatening and so revealing that few will try it. It will take time from mass evangelism and financial programs designed for immediate increase in church rolls. And not many people will hear your eloquence. Alone with a few deeply interested men and women, week after week, the holes in the mask of your education will show; and more particularly your own spiritual limitations and weaknesses will be revealed. Some will wander away. But if you are faithful and honest and keep your eyes on Christ and His will, I believe you will begin to experience together a new courage and a communicable enthusiasm, precisely *because* you are free to fail. Your strength and your hope is now in Christ and not in your own spiritual knowledge, ability, and results. As these men around you see the source of your life and theirs, they will begin to bring others to Christ. And the people these growing Christians bring into God's family will be born at a deeper level than they were, into an increasingly more committed and mature fellowship of men and women who are disciples becoming apostles for Christ.

The point is, if you genuinely want lay renewal in your church, I believe you will have to have somewhere in your own experience a living, growing fellowship of people who are being gently crushed into the wine of new life. This family will be the spiritual home, the true center of Christ's church, into which other people can be brought to be loved and reborn.

As I am completing these thoughts I remember years ago considering the kind of life which might be demanded of me if I made a consciously unreserved commitment of my future to Christ. I saw great spectres in my imagination of unpleasant things I would be required to do or be . . . all very pious and grim and a little frightening. Now, ten years later, I must smile. Because the strange fact of the matter is that when the time has come to say or do some of the things I had feared, I have been compelled to say or do them by a real and joyous desire to do so. Instead of grimness has come the freedom and joy of being able to accept myself as a self-centered sinner being won to Christ . . . day by day.

Finally, I was afraid that if I really cut the cord of the anchor which was tied to my self and began to venture forth in faith, God would send me to the mission field (which would of course mean Africa, India, or some remote place, since Christ said to be his witnesses to "the end of the earth"—(Acts 1:8)). But recently I have seen why it is that I have always thought of the "end of the earth" as some far-off place. I now realize that it is because the *center* of the world has always been *wherever I am*. But where then is the end of the earth from *God's* perspective?

If the heart which beat in Jesus Christ was in any sense the heart which throbs at the center of the universe, then the "end of the earth" from God's perspective may be wherever the influence from that heartbeat stops—in your own home, your own business, your own congregation. So it may be that Christ is calling those of us who have tasted of His new wine to stay at home, right where we are, and be wholly His people there. And perhaps for the first time in our lives we will find that we have truly . . . come Home.

Habitation of dragons

by KEITH MILLER

GUIDEPOSTS ASSOCIATES, INC.

Carmel, New York

*To Mary Allen, Emma, Gene, and
Floyd, each of whom gave invaluable
help and encouragement . . . without which, in the end, the dragons
might have written a book about me.*

To the Reader

Some years ago I began to look for books which would describe the kind of *inner* Christian life which would lead one to an *outer* vulnerable involvement with other people.

Occasionally, I would find a writer who dared to admit an inner problem with which I wrestled regularly. And the release I experienced in finding a fellow struggler was tremendous. To know that I am not alone with the shameful dragons I fight in my inner life is very encouraging. Somehow the knowledge that others face these problems makes them not quite so fearsome in their habitation in my mind. Paradoxically, I discovered that the more of my own self-centeredness and sin I see and confess to God, the more free I feel to relate to other people who have problems in the world.

The Christian life is a very positive but often a painful experience for me. God seems to urge me forward to grow and learn. And I want to go on. But I resist the truth about myself because it is painful and threatening to see my imperfections and to try to change . . . even for Him. This book is not meant to be a substitute for your own prayers and thoughts but only some footprints of a Christian wanderer on the inner journey who is finding tremendous hope in the midst of life.

I have written these pages for men and women who would like to try to spend a few minutes every day thinking and praying about the problems of the Christian way. The book was not designed to be read straight through, but one "day" at a time—either by individuals or study groups who are hoping they will be led beyond themselves to love others. The format is very simple. Traditionally, the principal ways Christians have sought to determine God's will for their lives have been: (1) In the Scriptures, (2) through prayer, (3) in the lives and writings of other men, and (4) through personal experience. So for each of 42 days I have described a personal problem, related it to the thought of an outstanding writer, prayed about the situation as I have tried to face it, and indicated a passage of Scripture which seems relevant. The issues and dilemmas included are some of those of a writer and speaker who is also a business consultant. They do not represent the "ideal," "average," or the "most acceptable" problems a Christian should have. I realize that some of them may be foreign to your life. Many of the experiences were taken directly from my journal, kept during the past 20 years. Actual names and descriptions in the stories have been changed in most cases.

The pronoun "I" is on almost every page. For this I have no apology, since these experiences and problems are part of my own life. I am not posing as the world's worst sinner, nor as its most humble saint. But I have used this personal form in the hope that what is written may serve as a kind of mirror in which some of you may see some aspects of your own inner lives with Christ.

The idea of self-examination and commitment taking place in a wilderness setting came from Jesus' 40 days in the desert after His baptism (Matthew 4:1–11; Mark 1:12,13). Traditionally, many churches have used the 40 days before Easter each year as a time for self-examination and redirection. If you would like to use this book for that period, you can begin with the first "Wednesday" in the book, and you will finish the last reading Easter morning.

The title is from a passage in the 35th chapter of Isaiah (KJV) in which the author tells us that one day the Lord will make that frightening and desolate place which is the habitation of dragons into a green new land, and through this land He will build a highway . . . which shall be called the way of holiness.

Keith Miller
Austin, Texas

Acknowledgments

Because of the spectrum of subjects covered here, several friends were good enough to read this manuscript in very rough form and give me specific suggestions concerning relevance and continuity. For this I am especially grateful to Brooks Goldsmith, Charles Sumners, Vester Hughes, Ann Hutchinson, Bruce Larson, Ralph Osborne, Leslie and Kristin Miller, and Gene Warr, who also helped me immeasurably in the selection of the Bible verses. Since I did not follow all their suggestions, I cannot blame these people for the shortcomings and mistakes you will find.

At one point, when the telephone and doorbell seemed about to swamp this project, our dear friends Loise and Joe Wessendorf called and suggested I go to their beautiful retreat center in central Texas to finish the writing. I did, and was deeply moved and refreshed by the time spent there.

Emma Ward patiently typed and retyped these pages and helped our editor, Floyd Thatcher, and my loving wife and best friend, Mary Allen, with detailed corrections and personal support.

I would also like to acknowledge the guiding Christian friendship of "Walter's bunch," the St. David's prayer therapy crew, and Bob Slocum, Richard Bauer and Douglas Harrell. Dick and Doug died during the time this manuscript was being written. Their clear-eyed facing of cancer and their own death not only affected this book but changed my life.

Contents

Habitation of Dragons

Then the eyes of the blind shall be opened,

    and the ears of the deaf unstopped;

Then shall the lame man leap as a hart,

    and the tongue of the dumb sing;

For in the wilderness shall the waters break out,

    and streams in the desert.

And the parched ground shall become a pool,

    and the thirsty land springs of water:

In the habitation of dragons, where each lay,

    shall be grass with reeds and rushes.

And a highway shall be there, and a way,

    and it shall be called The way of holiness . . .

Isaiah 35:5–8 (KJV)

Nothing Wasted

THE FEAR of failure has played a fascinating backstage role in my life. In looking across the years I can see that I have made a good many of my decisions on the basis of this fear.

As a boy, I remember choosing sports in which I was reasonably sure I could do well and avoiding those in which I was likely to be beaten. And it was not only sports. I made a good many choices on the basis of *"not* failing." This was true even though I was quite willing to start at the bottom and make mistakes of all kinds while learning the fundamentals of those activities I did choose.

As I grew up, I came to see that this insecurity is related to a deeper and more profound doubt about my masculine adequacy, which makes me overcompensate continually to prove myself. But the outward effect has been that I have had great difficulty in making decisions which involve risking my reputation. Although I was not conscious of it, I was afraid of failing because I pictured the consequences as being devastating. I should have made a vocational change years before I did, but I was afraid to risk it. "What if I didn't make it on my own? What if I failed?" So I stayed where I was, miserable, but afraid to take a chance, expecting that a great specter "failure" would somehow cripple me for life if I did. No amount of pointing to past accomplishments or acknowledged ability seemed to put this fear to rest. So I stayed where I was.

When I became a Christian, I knew that this kind of anxious behavior was certainly not the freedom and abundant life of which Christ spoke. But I still had the pattern of inner indecision and fear about my own future when I thought about stepping out on my own. Outwardly, I was very decisive in other areas, which served to hide my inner inadequacy in this one. But in my mind I knew I was a real prisoner when it came to risking a radical vocational change.

Several years later, through a series of circumstances which almost forced me to decide, I changed jobs. Then, within a period of less than five years I made five changes of occupation—each time feeling as if the new change were definitely in line with God's will as I could see it. Somehow this feeling helped me to risk failure. I know that some of our friends must have thought I was off my rocker and headed for disaster. But I was working hard and finding out a great deal about the various worlds through which we moved during those years.

The important thing I learned is that for a Christian *nothing* is wasted in this life: no bad decision, no vocational change, no personal failure. I am deeply interested in the communication of the gospel of Jesus Christ to modern man. And my four years of Business Administration training, as well as the fifteen years I spent in the oil exploration business, are in some ways more helpful to me in communicating with laymen now than the four years I spent doing graduate work in theological schools. Every directional choice which seemed to be wrong along the way was to become a kind of "drawbridge" which would let me into a specific vocational or social world later . . . worlds which would have been closed to me if I had gone directly into "the ministry."

When I broke my back and thought that I was going to be paralyzed from the neck down, when my parental family was destroyed by sickness and accident, and when I did not get a certain crucial promotion, such tragedies seemed so meaningless and wasteful. Yet these and other disappointments provided the only doorways I now have into the hearts and lives of struggling men and women. For many of them live with tragedy and disappointments and are also afraid to make decisions which involve risk. Finally, it was my inability to be able to control my circumstances which led me to begin to turn my life toward God.

Now I have less trouble making decisions than ever before in my life. I think this is partly because I know that even if I fail (and I never *want* to fail), that I will see how God meets a man in that particular kind of situation. The experience at least may help me to understand those people I will meet tomorrow or next year who will be going through the jungle of failure and dying to their images of success. And I have found a good bit of release from the fear of failure in this discovery that nothing has to be wasted in a life with God.

··+◆❖◆+··

"Much as I long to be out of here, I don't believe a single day has been wasted. What will come out of my time here it is too early to say. But something is bound to come out of it . . ."[1]

Dietrich Bonhoeffer
Prisoner for God

··+◆❖◆+··

Once when Mahatma Gandhi was twenty-four years old he was working as an attorney in South Africa. He boarded an overnight train with a first class ticket. At Maritzburg a white man got on, looked at Gandhi, and went to get two railroad officers. When they tried to get him to leave the first class compartment, he showed them his ticket and refused to move. Gandhi was thrown off the train onto the station platform at the next stop. Years later Dr. John R. Mott, an American missionary in India, asked Mahatma Gandhi what had been the most creative experiences in his life. And Gandhi told him about the experience at Maritzburg. For here it was that the mild little Indian's life was redirected to fight the ugliness of color prejudice with the most unusual weapons in history: love and non-violent resistance.[2]

Louis Fischer (paraphrased)
Gandhi

DEAR GOD, help me in my weakness not to be afraid to live and to try my wings in directions which seem right for me and my family. On the other hand, keep me from using this freedom to rationalize and run away from responsibility when the present situation gets rough. Help me to realize today that I am free either to stay or go, knowing that You can take the failures and mistakes resulting from my bad decisions and some day possibly turn them into wisdom and sensitivity in relations with other people. Pray for me, Lord, I do not know how to pray about success and failure. So often I have been wrong in determining that which I thought would be best for me.

"Likewise the Spirit helps us in our weakness; for we do not know how to pray as we ought, but the Spirit himself intercedes for us with sighs too deep for words. And he who searches the hearts of men knows what is the mind of the Spirit, because the Spirit intercedes for the saints according to the will of God.

"We know that in everything God works for good with those who love him, who are called according to his purpose."

Romans 8:26–28

The Incompleteness of "Total Honesty"
(Problem of Integrity No. 1)

IT WAS STILL very dark, but I was awake, having been disturbed by a bad dream. I was weeping because the dream had recalled an experience in my adolescence which was so painful that I thought I would never be free from its haunting presence. Several times over the years I had been bothered by this dream. And it always made me cringe, wanting to undo something I had done as a teenager.

This experience and its painful reliving over the years had changed my whole life, especially my views concerning integrity, love, and honesty in close relationships. And although I hated the memory and had prayed many times that God would erase it from my mind, there was no doubt that it had helped me as a husband, father, and friend.

It had happened at a boys' summer camp where I was a counselor after my freshman year in college. I was in charge of a cabin full of junior boys, about eight and nine years old. They were at the hero-worship age, and I really loved them. One boy, Mortey, an orphan from somewhere in eastern Oklahoma, was a particular favorite of mine. We became very close friends. He was in my canoe on the float trip and played the starring comedy role in the play I wrote and ramrodded as tribe coordinator. He was a cagey little performer and stole the show with his quick grasp of humor. Although they teased Mortey about his weight and the fact that he wore glasses, he was outgoing and had lots of old-fashioned guts and intelligence.

The little guy used to reach up and take my hand when we were walking alone, as if I were his dad. And I would look down at him and smile. He tended to be a little cocky about everything, including his relationship with me—though he never acted that way when he thought I was around.

At the end of eight weeks the time came for the camp awards. The counselors met to vote on the honor camper trophies—the most important symbols of acceptance and success a boy could win. When the preliminary weeding out had been done, two boys remained in the race for junior honor camper: Mortey and Bobby. Wanting to have integrity, I decided I was so biased I could not vote, but when the ballots had been counted, both boys had the same number. I had to vote to break the tie.

At that time in my life I was an obsessive compulsive on the inside, and a joking character on the outside. But I had been taught that absolute integrity was the highest value; and, when decisions which seemed to concern my integrity were to be made, I really strained to do the right thing.

As I looked at these two boys and their camp records, I tried to be objective. Bobby was a much better athlete and had broken some records, but Mortey definitely had the edge in the human understanding department. They had both helped their tribes by winning contests and by being friendly kids. It was easy to see why the vote had been tied. I was miserable. Little Mortey had done a great job . . . but he *was* a little cocky, and he did have a few faults I knew about. This definitely gave Bobby a slight edge. Everyone knew how close we had been; and if I voted for Mortey, I was afraid the other counselors would think I was voting for him because of our friendship. It was strange that such a trivial thing could have been so momentous, but my whole integrity seemed to be on the line, and I felt sort of sick at my stomach. I did not want the responsibility of deciding.

My hesitation over the simple decision was delaying the meeting, and the other counselors became irritated. Under this pressure I decided—against Mortey. And we went on.

Only inside I didn't go on. I knew that although I had been honest, I had somehow been wrong. While sitting there, I got the idea that I ought to level with Mortey about what had happened. I tried to dismiss the thought, but it kept coming back. And I felt I *had* to tell him the truth "in order to have integrity" in the situation.

On the last morning at camp, as all the boys were getting on the bus, Mortey came up to me. Everyone was yelling for him to hurry. His face was streaked with tears, and it was obvious that he had been crying and did not want me to know. As we walked away from the others, I told him how much our friendship meant to me. I went on to tell him how close he had come to being elected honor camper—that in fact the vote had been a tie. His eyes got very wide, and I continued in my nineteen-year-old total honesty, "I hadn't voted up 'til that time, Mortey, because everyone knows that you and I are such close friends. But they made me vote then . . . and I voted for Bobby." As I started to explain why I had done it, the look on his face caught me completely off guard. I will never forget it. It haunts me still, because I saw the look of a soul betrayed by his dearest friend. In an instant I saw how wrong I had been and why. This little boy really loved me. And I realized that he *had* done a much finer job than Bobby at camp. But because Mortey had loved me, he had revealed his faults as well as his good points to me, and I had used this knowledge to judge and condemn him (from his perspective).

He just stood there and stared at me in disbelief. After his dad had let him down by leaving his mother, he had trusted me. I had the chance to give him all he had ever wanted, but I had tossed it to another boy in a different tribe, whom I hardly knew. He covered his face with his hands and ran toward the bus. I tried to grab him, to explain my feelings; but he broke loose and, wriggling between the last few campers, disappeared onto the bus. The door closed and the bus pulled out. I ran along beside it, hunting for Mortey in the windows. But all the other kids were pressed against them, and I didn't see him at all. In the midst of the shouting and singing of the camp loyalty song, Mortey rode out of my life in a cloud of dust.

It was years later, after I became a Christian and began to understand myself and my problems more clearly, that I began to see the trap "honesty" can be. It had become my highest value: "honesty at any cost." This meant that I *worshiped* honesty. In my struggle to decide who should be honor camper, I had been so intent on maintaining my own integrity that the broader values in the judging situation had escaped me. And in any case, I was blind to the consequences of trying to clear my own skirts with Mortey by telling him all—not realizing that a nine-year-old boy could not understand me. Yet maybe he *did* understand me and that was what broke his heart.

For this little boy saw the world through a different set of eyes than I did. It was to be almost ten years before I began to put myself into the hands of One who saw life in the same way that Mortey did. For in his world there was a higher

value than raw honesty with which to judge people . . . and
that value is love.

······

"If he actually did it (was honest) for the sake of
having a good conscience, he would become a Pharisee
and cease to be a truly moral person. I think that even
saints did not care for anything other than simply to
serve God, and I doubt that they ever had it in mind to
become saints. If that were the case, they would have
become only perfectionists rather than saints."[3]

Viktor E. Frankl
Man's Search for Meaning

······

LORD, help me to realize the limited nature of my ability to
judge the total circumstances in any human encounter. Forgive me for being blinded by needs for integrity and putting
my adolescent desire for rightness ahead of Mortey's need
for love. But, God, thank You for teaching me through that
little boy the importance of the kind of loving loyalty You
have for us which transcends all your gifts including faith,
and even Your judgment of that which we deserve.

······

"If I speak in the tongues of men and of angels, but
have not love, I am a noisy gong or a clanging cymbal.
And if I have prophetic powers, and understand all
mysteries and all knowledge, and if I have all faith, so
as to remove mountains, but have not love, I am nothing."

I Corinthians 13:1–2

A Case for Purity

I AM CONTINUALLY amazed at some people who have been "born and raised" in the Christian faith, who tell me that I should talk about "victories" instead of problems. Last weekend I was conducting a conference for a group of deacons from a large church. It just happened that two of the witnesses I brought along had both been through a tough problem with adultery. This being a men's group, the witnesses in the opening session had talked about how rough it was to wrestle with the problems of extra-marital sex and how their despair had driven them to take a serious look toward God. But the discussion that followed was stilted and centered around church and organizational problems.

After the meeting that night the minister cornered me and was pretty upset. "I'm afraid you have the wrong group, Mr. Miller," he began. "These men I brought up here are converted Christians, deacons in my church. I know them all personally. If you keep dealing with these kinds of personal problems, I'm afraid you will lose our group's attention altogether."

I called our team together and told them we really had to pray, because the minister thought the participants were offended with us. After the team went to bed, I stayed in the office of the retreat center thinking of what we could do to recover our communication in the morning with a program which might meet the needs of thirty converted deacons. As I sat there alone late at night, there was a knock on the door. It was one of the deacons. After a long talk and prayer with this man, he left and went to bed, only to be followed by another, and then another. Five of the deacons came in that night to confess the same kinds of sex problems the witnesses had mentioned. They wanted to know if we honestly thought there was forgiveness and freedom for them—since they were committed Christians and yet had these same difficulties. I told them that I thought that there was forgiveness. And in each case after their confession we thanked God for His forgiveness and for a new chance.

The next day we faced a happy bunch of men. They were clustered around the two witnesses and were very warm and friendly. The men were open and seemed to care about each other. Their conversation now centered around how to reach other people in their town and help them to find freedom in Christ.

The minister was ecstatic to see his deacons befriending their "weaker brothers," the witnesses. When he pointed this out to me, I had to agree that here was indeed a group of deacons with an unusual degree of involvement.

The group got together before leaving. And when the minister found out what had actually happened, he said he was shocked at first, then thoughtful, and then in some way relieved that they did not have to pretend to each other any more that there are no serious problems for the committed Christian man to confess. And he thanked the two lay witnesses who thought they had failed.

..+◄◙▹+·

"For him who confesses, shams are over and realities
have begun; he has exteriorized his rottenness. If he has
not actually got rid of it, he at least no longer smears it
over with a hypocritical show of virtue—he lives at least
upon a basis of veracity . . . The complete decay of the
practice of confession in Anglo-Saxon communities is a
little hard to account for . . . One would think that in
more men the shell of secrecy would have had to open,
the pent-in abscess to burst and gain relief, even though
the ears that heard the confession were unworthy."[4]

William James
*The Varieties of Religious
Experience*

Private confession to a brother . . . "is useful, even
necessary, and I would not have it abolished. Indeed, I
rejoice that it exists in the church of Christ, for it is a
cure without equal for distressed consciences. For when
we have laid bare our conscience to our brother and
privately made known to him the evil that lurked within,
we receive from our brother's lips the word of comfort
spoken by God himself. And, if we accept this in faith,
we find peace in the mercy of God speaking to us
through our brother."[5]

Martin Luther
Works, Vol. 36

..+◄◙▹+·

LORD, I don't know who started the notion that being a Christian, or a deacon, or even a bishop somehow seals one's life
off from the problems of the world. But I wish You would tell
whoever it was to stop saying it. Teach us to accept Your
forgiveness and the power to change our lives. But when we
trip and fall, help us to confess our sins, get up, and go on

loving and helping people in Your name. Keep us from being naïve whitened sepulchers who cannot accept the stark fact of failure in our lives . . . and therefore Your forgiveness available to us through Jesus Christ.

·+‹❈›+·

"If we say we have no sin, we deceive ourselves, and the truth is not in us. If we confess our sins, he is faithful and just, and will forgive our sins and cleanse us from all unrighteousness."

I John 1:8,9

"You Don't Listen to
Me Any More!"

Y OU DON'T listen to me any more!" I blurted out, right in the middle of a sentence I was "delivering."

"Why, I *do too*," Mary Allen answered in what seemed like genuine surprise.

But I did not believe her. After a week of traveling on a speaking trip, I am usually a highly tuned listener to individuals with whom I have been counseling. And I can usually spot it when someone is not paying attention to what *I* am saying. When I first started traveling, Mary Allen pumped me for details about each trip as soon as I got home. Often I did not feel like "replaying" the meeting, but she wanted to hear, so I would. But now something had happened. She still asked about the trips, but then seemed to get diverted by almost any kind of interruption, often just as I was getting into something which was very exciting to me. This really bugged me, and I would get furious. If she didn't want to listen, then why did she ask? . . . and then not pay attention. Maybe she was getting bored with me. After all, we had been married seventeen years.

Anyway, I was furious when this happened yesterday. I

had just come home from a seven-day trip. The two meetings I had attended were made up of very sharp couples. Although many of the people did not agree with some of the things I was saying and doing, they gave me the great compliment of listening to me. In counseling sessions and social visits between the larger meetings, people who came to see me could not have been more attentive, and I was conscious of being very open and receptive to each of them.

But when I got home, here was this seeming indifference. Being a neurotic, I conjured up reasons for Mary Allen's behavior, all of which boiled down to the facts that (1) she was not interested in that which I was doing and (2) she was not interested in me. And after a couple of hours of unexplained resentment and cutting remarks—which had the desired effects of making us both miserable—I let my problem out in the open.

Following the initial expression of feelings back and forth, we began to talk about what had happened. Being so mad at her, I had a hard time hearing what she was saying. But one thing echoed in my mind as I drove toward the office later: "When you come home from these speaking trips you act like a spoiled king!"

That hurt! And particularly because I had the sneaking suspicion that it just might be true—although it had not occurred to me before that my behavior and attitudes had changed upon returning from trips during the past couple of years, at least not in a *negative* way.

As I thought about this, I wondered how many lay speakers, ministers, doctors, bank presidents—people who get lots of personal attention and affirmation in their vocational lives —I wondered how many such men begin unconsciously to behave like spoiled kings without even knowing that it is happening. I wondered how many other men begin unconsciously to expect their wives and families to hang on their words and attend to their needs with the same speed and solicitousness their hosts at meetings or their secretaries do? I started not to write this because it is difficult for me to accept this about myself. Since I consciously want it not to be true, I would like to deny it to myself, and especially to you. But I am afraid it is true.

I realized that one of the things which makes it so bad—and I think may even exaggerate it in the eyes of a wife—is the fact that important unshared experiences often separate people. That is, when I have been off to a stimulating seminar alone, I often make the mistake of coming home and very excitedly telling Mary Allen about a "fantastic place," or person, or group, which has changed my life. In one sense she is glad. But in another sense, the experience which she did not share separates us, because I am implying that I am "going on" due to what happened to me. And since she was not present, there is an implication that I am leaving her behind—or perhaps an unconscious fear on her part that I might—even though that is not what I am saying or thinking.*

All this does not mean that I am suddenly going to quit talking about trips and conferences when I come home. That would really cause problems. But I am going to attempt to be more thoughtful concerning the *way* I talk about them. I hope I will not forget to find out first what has been going on at home to laugh or cry about while I have been away. And I am going to try not to expect a woman with two teenage daughters —and a third on the teenage threshold—to suddenly stop the world in which she has been operating alone for a week, to cheer at my recital of the great time I have had (away from home responsibilities) as an "honored guest" somewhere.

---

* Of course this situation can be reversed in cases where the wife is the conference-going religious fanatic of the family.

"But I am sure my readers understand the subtle temptation which assails me: that of trying to be the personage I am expected to be. It slips in disguised as an honest concern for the proper fulfilment of my vocation. . . .

"In order not to disappoint them I ought to tell them only of my positive experiences. In fact they are always disconcerted at first when I speak of my own difficulties, doubts and failings. But they soon come to see that this atmosphere of truth brings us closer and binds us together. My experience of the power of God means more to them than it would if they thought me a quite different sort of person from themselves."[6]

Paul Tournier
The Meaning of Persons

LORD, forgive me for my self-centered blindness to my own insensitivity. Give me the insight to see the effect of my real behavior on other people and on You. And then, Lord, please give me the courage and strength to confess my sin and change my actions. Thank You, God, that You are in the life-changing business.

"For by the grace given to me I bid every one among you not to think of himself more highly than he ought to think, but to think with sober judgment, each according to the measure of faith which God has assigned him."

Romans 12:3

Do It Unto Me

AFTER TEN years of making the attempt to commit my life to God, most of my close personal relationships had been deeply affected. I still could not keep them all straightened out, but had found an open style of relating that made confession, forgiveness, beginning again—and sometimes change—possible with my family and close associates.

But as I watched the news and talked to college students and black groups, the question began to plague me: "How does this openness lead Christians out into the world to become vulnerably involved with Christ in the *social* agony around us?" I couldn't find any rules for this. But some of us began getting involved with people who had real material needs as a result of a small group which meets at 6:30 on Monday mornings.

We had started this group to begin to learn in a safe, loving atmosphere how to communicate about the hope and meaning we were finding inside our lives, where we had been so alone with our faith. This was not an "honesty cult" in which to confess our lurid sins, nor was it a pietistic clique; but it was a place to begin facing openly the troubles and problems we had in living, working, and praying, which kept us from being God's people and doing His will.

As the months went by, we tried to help each other to investigate and discover the shape our lives and ministries might take in our own community. That was when I began to become acutely conscious of some of the social problems we have. And as we started to share this inward journey with Christ and with each other, some of us were led beyond our own horizons and out into the world in ways we never could have anticipated.

One of the men in this group was named George. He is a successful and wealthy home builder and real estate developer. But George had spent part of his youth in an orphan's home and knew what it was like to have very little. He had made a commitment of his life to Christ a few years earlier and had begun to relearn to live. One morning George came into the group and was very thoughtful. "I woke up at four o'clock this morning," he said, "and I couldn't go back to sleep. I was praying and discovered an amazing thing—I love niggers!" George had tears in his eyes. Having been raised as a southern boy, he didn't see anything incongruous about what he had said. He went on, "But if I love them, I guess God would want me to do something to help them wouldn't He?" We supposed so. "I would like for you to pray that I'll be able to find out what I can do to help Christ with the race situation *here in town.*" And we did pray that, although I felt a restlessness in my own life as we prayed.

The next week George came to the meeting excited, but uncertain. "They've asked me to serve on the human relations commission, and they want me to come out with a public statement in favor of open housing. I went around to the other realtors in town and they said, 'We think that would be a great thing for *you* to do, George,' but none of them would go along on the statement. So I checked a national realtor's study and found out that, in the price range of my homes, if a black family moves in, the surrounding property values decline at once and quite a bit." He stopped a minute. "What I found out was that this public stand on open housing might ruin me financially." We wrestled with George in his dilemma that morning and finally told him that whatever he decided, we hoped that he would not make the statement because of guilt, but only if he thought it was God's will for him.

The following week the whole business came to a head. George said he had been looking into the problem and praying about what to do when he remembered something Elton Trueblood had told our group a few weeks before. It was the old story about the man who had the crazy notion that he wanted to walk across Niagara Falls on a tightrope pushing a wheelbarrow with a man in it. He set up two poles in his backyard, stretched a tightrope between them, and practiced every day for a year—first with a balance bar, then without it, then with a wheelbarrow, and finally he added a load of 175 pounds of bricks. And he never fell off the wire. His next-door neighbor watched every evening, and the crowds got larger each day as the time drew near. The press picked up the story, and when the big moment came, a huge throng was on hand. The fellow with the wheelbarrow appeared to be a little nervous as he stood looking out. across the wire. He turned to his faithful neighbor and asked, "Joe, do you believe I can do it?"

Slapping him confidently on the back Joe said, "I absolutely believe you can. I bet a tenth of this year's income on you."

The performer looked out over the falls and then asked once more, "Joe, do you *really* believe?"

Joe said seriously, "I *really believe.*"

"Fine," the other fellow replied, *"you're* my man. Get in the wheelbarrow."

Then George said quietly to the rest of us in the group, "This week the Lord said to me 'George, if you trust Me with your future, get in the wheelbarrow on this race thing.' And I did."

This is not a story with a happy ending. It cost George about a hundred thousand dollars the first year and some painful rejection in our city. We don't know yet how much more it will cost him. But something happened to several of us in that group about that same time. Two ministers granted use of their church educational wing for a head start program downtown during the week. And there is now a free medical clinic in that church being run by an interdenominational group for poor people who can't qualify for other help. I started to try to talk to black groups and learn about the real issues in the racial struggles. And several of us began to be haunted about ways we might help Christ with the poor people in our city.

This beginning to move out, beyond my own personal and business associations, took place for me because a man let a few of us share in his struggle against a life-long prejudice, and we watched him—afraid, wonderful—as he climbed in the wheelbarrow for Jesus Christ . . . and for some black men and women and little children—who will never know.

I do not know how much we can do, and sometimes I am afraid of the hostility of people whose backgrounds and circumstances are different from my own. Sometimes the race and poverty situations seem so hopeless that I just want to run away and forget them. But I pray that I will not. Because as I get closer to people who appear to be different from me, I find that most of the real differences are in my mind. And as I take small, specific steps to go and do things which need doing, I realize that Christ is probably not as concerned with measuring the magnitude of my effectiveness . . . as with whether or not I go.

·+ ◆◄▒►◆ +·

"Faith without ethical consequences is a lie. Good works must necessarily follow faith. God does not need our sacrifices but he has, nevertheless, appointed a representative to receive them, namely our neighbor. The neighbor always represents the invisible Christ."[7]

J. S. Whale
Christian Doctrine

·+ ◆◄▒►◆ +·

Lord, thank You that You have not called upon me to be all-powerful or omnipresent but only to be a part of a larger family, a team. Forgive me when I try to pitch, catch, hit, and manage the entire team all at the same time. But help me to have enough sense and courage to play the position You have given me in this changing world, even if it's not in the "big leagues." Somehow in my megalomania it is hard for me to participate when I cannot lead or when I cannot at least see the hope of solving the whole problem through my efforts. Help me to learn the value to You of a "cup of cold water" where it's really needed and how to use a bucket to wash some tired smelly feet—without an audience.

·+ ◆◄▒►◆ +·

"Then the King will say to those at his right hand, 'Come, O blessed of my Father, inherit the kingdom prepared for you from the foundation of the world; for I was hungry and you gave me food, I was thirsty and you gave me drink, I was a stranger and you welcomed me, I was naked and you clothed me, I was sick and you visited me, I was in prison and you came to me.' Then the righteous will answer him, 'Lord, when did we see thee hungry and feed thee, or thirsty and give thee drink? And when did we see thee a stranger and welcome thee, or naked and clothe thee? And when did we see thee sick or in prison and visit thee?' And the King will answer them, 'Truly, I say to you, as you did it to one of the least of these my brethern, you did it to me.' "

Jesus Christ
Matthew 25:34–40

Change of Life

L AST NIGHT I visited with a friend. He is younger than I, but he looks like a tired old man, and he is very sick physically. I can still see his haunted eyes. The urgency he now feels about his health made me starkly aware of the reality of my own aging. As I thought about life and its changes, I realized what a strange little creature I am. One minute I am a big virile male with the world by the tail. But I can be deflated in an instant by the first sign of diminishing sexual virility or genuine rejection. I get depressed and insecure sometimes and find myself imagining and doing all kinds of irrational things to bolster my fading youth.

I think it is unfortunate that we are not taught somewhere in our growing up that we men also go through a transition period psychologically comparable to "change of life" in women.* Life seems to be slipping by and it is not quite what we thought it would be. There is no longer that limitless sea of time ahead of us in this pilgrimage in which we find fulfillment. A kind of fear sets in.

I have never seen it this clearly before. All we usually feel

---

* "It is now well established that men as well as women go through an involutional period." Kisker, George W., *The Disorganized Personality* (New York: McGraw-Hill, 1964), p. 377.

is that our wives are getting demanding or bossy or unreasonable. And there are more things that make us nervous, restless, and fearful than there used to be. But it is kind of comforting to know that all of this is just a part of the process of living. I don't know what I would do if I had come to this point in my life without God and fellow strugglers like you with whom I can hope to find acceptance. Of course, sometimes when I look at the problems of old age and death, I wonder if Christianity is a cruel joke and we are deluding ourselves and missing our only chance to live it up. And a panicky feeling stirs in my chest.

But at such times, my mind scans all the world's bright opportunities and material signs of fulfillment for an option to this life of faith, and I ask myself, "Of all the things you have tried and tasted, what is more real than this relationship with the living God and His people?" And whatever else that has seemed important fades away. So I smile and sigh; and again with a deep sense of release, I offer my life to Jesus Christ and to the finding of His place for me in His family. This is not done in desperation. But after years of trying to find something to hang my life on, I have discovered that the greatest achievements and philosophies about which I have known are poor seconds to the clear hope and the sense of ultimate acceptance and caring I have found in this experimental life in Christ. And I am grateful that although the problems and distresses of living may lay me low, they cannot separate me from the love of God. In such moments I realize that I have discovered a good direction for my life. And I get up and go to work a happier person . . . as I am going to do right now! Have a good day!

·⊹+✦❊❈❊✦+⊹·

"Proper recognition and appreciation of normal instincts leads the young person into life and entangles him with fate, thus involving him in life's necessities and the consequent sacrifices and efforts through which his character is developed and his experience matured. For the mature person, however, the continued expansion of life is obviously not the right principle, because the descent towards life's afternoon demands simplification, limitation, and intensification—in other words, individual culture. A man in the first half of life with its biological orientation can usually, thanks to the youthfulness of his whole organism, afford to expand his life and make something of value out of it. But the man in the second half of life is oriented towards culture, the diminishing powers of his organism allowing him to subordinate his instincts to cultural goals. Not a few are wrecked during the transition from the biological to the cultural sphere. Our collective education makes practically no provision for this transitional period. Concerned solely with the education of the young, we disregard the education of the adult, of whom it is always assumed—on what grounds who can say?—that he needs no more education. There is an almost total lack of guidance for this extraordinarily important transition from the biological to the cultural attitude, for the transition of energy from the biological form into the cultural form."[8]

Carl Jung
The Collected Works, Vol. 8

Faith . . . "is a great art and doctrine, which no saint has learned and fathomed fully unless he has found himself in despair, in the anguish of death, or in extreme peril."[9]

Martin Luther
Works, Vol. XXIII

DEAR LORD, thank You for the signposts of physical change and death which force me to see the frail and transient nature of my life without You. I pray that in times of health and success I will not forget You and turn away. Give me the courage to face the stark realities of life and help me to move through each stage of development with a perspective of wisdom and joy instead of fear, knowing that You will be with me.

·•◄✦▐▶✦•·

"Who shall separate us from the love of Christ? Shall tribulation, or distress, or persecution, or famine, or nakedness, or peril, or sword? As it is written, 'For thy sake we are being killed all the day long; we are regarded as sheep to be slaughtered.' No, in all these things we are more than conquerors through him who loved us. For I am sure that neither death, nor life, nor angels, nor principalities, nor things present, nor things to come, nor powers, nor height, nor depth, nor anything else in all creation, will be able to separate us from the love of God in Christ Jesus our Lord."

Romans 8:35–39

The Critical Eye

H E WAS an excellent speaker," I heard myself saying sincerely, "but I thought he had a real need to let us know how much he had read, and I wondered if this got in people's way as they listened to him."

I was talking to Mary Allen on the way home from hearing a brilliant and winsome Christian speaker at a meeting. We both responded to him as a person, but I had felt uneasy during his lecture.

This morning when I was going through my prayers and came to "confession," I found myself saying, "God, forgive me for tearing down our friend last night. He is a fine Christian communicator and I am very grateful that he can do things I cannot."

As I said these words of confession, I saw why I needed to confess. I have a habit of subtly undermining people who are better than I am at doing the things I do. At a conscious level I am deeply grateful for anyone who is an effective Christian communicator. But if he is speaking to the same group I am trying to reach and if he has a different style from mine, I must be threatened somehow—as if people may think the other man's way is right and mine is wrong. This has not been a conscious reaction, but in looking back across the years I can see that it has been true.

Now, when I catch myself subtly criticizing a talented Christian communicator, I hope I will be able to see the reason my sharp little eyes have detected a chink in his armor so that I can *truly* be thankful that he is a spokesman for our common Lord.

·•✦◄§◊►◆·•

"Thou wilt never be an inwardly religious and devout man unless thou pass over in silence the shortcomings of thy fellow men, and diligently examine thine own weaknesses."[10]

Thomas à Kempis
The Imitation of Christ

". . . no one can get rid of the spirit of judgment by an effort of the will. As long as I am obsessed by a friend's fault which has shocked me and made me reproach him, no matter how much I say to myself; 'I do not wish to judge him,' I judge him none the less. But the spirit of judgment evaporates as soon as I become conscious of my own faults and speak freely of them to my friend, as he speaks to me of those which make him reproach himself.

". . . A man's judgment of another depends more on the one judging and on his passions than on the one being judged and his conduct."[11]

Paul Tournier
Guilt and Grace

·•✦◄§◊►◆·•

God, sometimes I can't imagine how You can put up with me. I tell You one minute that I love You with all my heart, and *mean* it. But the next hour I am murdering a fellow Christian by undermining what he has done, by subtly criticizing him and calling attention away from his message about You to his weaknesses, which I seem to be an expert at locating. Forgive me, and give me a new start right now. Help me to keep observing and learning by other men's mistakes as well as my own. But give me the security to affirm them for the helpful things they say about You, rather than subtly attacking their personalities and thus indirectly Your attempts to love men through them.

··+·‹‡⋮‡›·+··

"Why do you pass judgment on your brother? Or you, why do you despise your brother? For we shall all stand before the judgment seat of God; for it is written, 'As I live, says the Lord, every knee shall bow to me, and every tongue shall give praise to God.' . . . Then let us no more pass judgment on one another, but rather decide never to put a stumbling block or hindrance in the way of a brother."

Romans 14:10–13

True Grit?

THIS MORNING I woke up from a dream with a scene still vivid in my imagination. I was reliving a terrifying day in my childhood—a day which changed my life. There I was, standing in line in the first grade room trying to appear cool and unperturbed. But when the first little boy screamed and struggled to get away from the doctor who was giving the shots, my heart pounded so loudly I was afraid everyone could hear it. I even hummed softly to be sure they did not. Struggling against a terrifying urge to run out the door, I tried to appear casual by looking out the window at the white billowing clouds in the Spring sky. Other kids were making sniffling noises as if they were about to tune up and cry also. I was hoping they would, so maybe the teacher would call this whole thing off.

When I glanced toward the front of the room to see what was happening, my mother, who was a volunteer helper, spoke quietly to the doctor and then came back in the line to where I was standing. She bent over and whispered in my ear, "We want you to come up and take your shot now to show the other boys and girls how to be brave. It really doesn't hurt much."

I was terrified but also very pleased to be the one chosen as an example of courage. So I walked up to the doctor, calmly rolled up my sleeve, and stuck out my arm (as if I were only shaking hands—instead of about to get the needle).

I smiled as I remembered how proud my mother had been of me. She told my dad and older brother at dinner that night about my performance, and she mentioned my "courage" to a friend over the telephone. Somehow the die was cast. I *had* to be strong and courageous.

The only trouble was: I was not. I was afraid . . . of lots of things. But I acted courageously because I was more afraid of being found out than of the outward "dangers" and threats of life. So a pattern was established—one which caused me to be very anxious about possible exposure and made me feel inadequate inside, regardless of how well I performed in the arena of real life. I remember the paradoxical feelings once of being elected president of my high school class, making the ball team, and feeling very inadequate—all at the same time.

Then, the day came when I really understood that I am acceptable to God because of *His* loving and forgiving nature and not because of *my* ability or courage. I was overwhelmed. It was too good to be true. When I started to try to find His will as it impinged on my abilities and circumstances, I began to be free to admit my hidden fears and inadequacies to others who were afraid. Gradually, I started to reveal my inner self to God and to people, and some of them revealed themselves to me. I discovered some strange things about courage and inadequacy. Having always thought of those towering men who had a calm exterior in the face of danger as being unafraid, I was certain that some of them would think I was a chicken-hearted phony if they knew how I felt.

But the truth seems to be that many of them are scared, too, and have learned to hide their fears even from themselves. In fact I have discovered that the strongest people I know, the ones I would really want beside me in any real trouble or danger, are those who know that they are afraid, can admit it, and yet are willing to take risks for God and other people.

I don't know how or when it happened, but I am not nearly as afraid of people now as I once was. Possibly, this is because my greatest fear was not of real problems and threats, but of being found inadequate and rejected. Now I can sometimes risk revealing to others what seems to be more truly my real self. When they see "the frightened little boy" that I sometimes am inside and do not run away or laugh at me, I can more nearly believe their acceptance and affirmation when they offer it. Before I could not.

It seems to me that it is often very helpful to others to be strong and *not* reveal one's fear in the face of danger. But when the danger is over or when someone asks, it is strengthening to know that others were afraid too.

Somehow I think this paradox is near the heart of the kind of life presented in the gospel. God seems to be offering to use weak men and women who feel inadequate and incomplete to demonstrate in their courage a vulnerable kind of love and understanding the world seldom sees in the "strong and mighty ones."

··+·

"The adventurous life is not one exempt from fear, but on the contrary one that is lived in full knowledge of fears of all kinds, one in which we go forward in spite of our fears. Many people have the utopian idea that others are less afraid than they are, and they feel therefore that they are inferior. All men are afraid, even desperately afraid. If they think they are exempt from fear, that is because they have repressed their fears. Fear is part of human nature."[12]

Paul Tournier
The Adventure of Living

·+ ◆◎◎◆ +·

LORD, thank You that in a paradoxical way the power revealed through human personality is seen to be more clearly Yours when it inhabits an otherwise weak person. Help me today to learn to depend more on Your strength and acceptance for the source of my courage instead of the flimsy shield of my confident mask.

·+ ◆◎◎◆ +·

". . . 'My grace is all you need; power comes to its full strength in weakness.' I shall therefore prefer to find my joy and pride in the very things that are my weakness; and then the power of Christ will come and rest upon me. Hence I am well content, for Christ's sake, with weakness, contempt, persecution, hardship, and frustration; for when I am weak, then I am strong."

Jesus Christ and the Apostle Paul
II Corinthians 12:9, 10 (NEB)

An Offensive Way to Hide

YESTERDAY I was miserable. I was cross and unreasonable with my family, and yet I desperately needed their love and acceptance. This usually means that I feel insecure about myself in some area—my work, my future, the children's happiness. But instead of facing my fears and anxieties, I become a gruff independent critic of the scene around me . . . at those points at which it touches my self-imposed solitude. My responses are cynical. And I point out the selfish or thoughtless aspects of everyone else's behavior in order to correct them, for their own good, of course. In short, I am obnoxious.

But inside, behind the barrage of rejection I am pouring out over my family, is a miserable person who does not understand why he is so intent on fouling his own nest. At such times I desperately want to be loved—in spite of the fact that I know that I do not deserve it.

It happened again yesterday. And last night I could not stop it. But before I went to sleep I was able to tell Mary Allen that I was sorry I was being so mean and that I did not consciously want to be. After telling her, I realized what the cause was. Yesterday morning, after meeting with you, I had a personal crisis about my own future and let Mary Allen see

50

the fear and immaturity I still have about my performance—
a fear with which I have been stuck since childhood. Since I
thought that specter had been buried and had said so, I was
disappointed in myself and had felt very vulnerable when
Mary Allen had seen my weakness. Then I guess I must have
unconsciously wanted to hurt her because I was so frustrated
at not being able to change my own feelings. At least I wanted
to get the spotlight off that particular fault of mine. This was
true in spite of the fact that she had been very understanding
and loving, and I had appreciated it. But I guess way down
inside I could not believe she loved me in my weakness—
after all, I couldn't even love myself.

And I saw that *this* was the deeper issue. When I am
unacceptable to myself, I often try to raise a furor of negative
reactions and signals, evidently hoping that in the confusion
no one will notice my weakness. You might call it the
"skunk" system. As everyone knows, when a skunk gets in
trouble, he puts out a cloud of horrible odor that the other
animals all know will stick to them if it gets on them. So
everyone else scrambles for cover, and when the "smoke"
clears, the skunk has walked to safety.

Don't feel superior if you do not handle your vulnerability
in this way. One of our little girls likes the "turtle" method,
which is simply to pull in her head and withdraw. After
everyone tries to sniff around and bring her out, we all walk
away, and she has arrived at a safe "place" in which she can
mope or feel sorry for herself in peace. Having checked with
several people, it seems that this method is more popular than
that of the skunk. But unfortunately I find it very difficult to
make a turtle shell out of a skunk skin.*

·+◄◙▐▸+·

---

* It is astounding how many times skunks and turtles marry.

"How often we hide behind masks and hug delusions with compulsive passion because we are afraid to be known, to be loved—but in the nearness of real, deep, substantial love we run back to our masks of isolation, shallowness, and safety in terror of being revealed and accepted. We hide ourselves in acts of passion; we bury love under false prudence; we substitute biological pleasures for the divine wonder and peril of love; we surround ourselves with cold, icy barriers to defend the smug self from being shattered by love.

"It is easier to snub another ('snuff the light of his life out of our life') than to love. And so we indulge in spiritual assassination in order to protect our own convenience."[13]

William McNamara
The Art of Being Human

··+◄▌▐►+··

LORD, help me to keep short accounts with You by confessing my sins and fears as soon as I am aware of them. I don't want to hurt everyone around me in order to cover up my own needs and insecurities. Thank You that although I am more aware of my faults and incompleteness than I ever have been, I feel a strange buoyancy and strength in being able to live with the problems out in the world in my relationships. I don't understand why I am so ready to point out the faults of others as a defense to hide my own, but I would certainly appreciate some help as I begin to concentrate on not doing it.

··+◄▌▐►+··

"Judge not, that you be not judged. For with the judgment you pronounce you will be judged, and the measure you give will be the measure you get. Why do you see the speck that is in your brother's eye, but do not notice the log that is in your own eye? Or how can you say to your brother, 'Let me take the speck out of your

eye,' when there is a log in your own eye? You hypo-
crite, first take the log out of your own eye, and then you
will see clearly to take the speck out of your brother's
eye."

Matthew 7:1–5.

The Difficult Is *Good?*

THIS MORNING I woke up feeling very uneasy with a strong urge to "escape." Suddenly I sat up in bed wondering, "What's the matter with you?" I thought about our lives and my job and realized that things are going well. We are all healthy and have enough to eat. Mary Allen and the children do not have any major problems. I am in the midst of writing this book. But I have the feeling that it is dull and you will not read it—or if you do, you will think I am naïve. So I will have to go through the agony of reworking the manuscript again to try to reproduce in writing the pictures which I see in my mind. And this is very difficult for me.

At this point I saw my problem. For some reason I was trying to avoid writing, the very thing I love to do. Why? As I thought back over my life, I realized that I have often avoided things I really wanted to do, just because they were difficult. I remember as a skinny little boy wanting to have a well proportioned physique. But I would do almost anything, including feigning sickness on occasion, to avoid heavy muscle-building work around our yard. I love to learn, and yet in school I avoided studying as long as possible.

Later, as an adult, I strongly resisted the notion of committing my life to God. Although I was strongly attracted to the idea and suspected that it was the better way, the suggestion of "total commitment" made me angry and was repelling. Such a commitment would no doubt fill my life with difficulties and force me to examine my true motivations at every turn. I was convinced that I would have to give up the normal joys and goals of life.

Throughout my life a strong desire has often forced me to overcome my resistance and try the more difficult thing: to begin doing the calisthenics, work, study in school, and finally, to become a Christian. In each case, when I chose what appeared to be the difficult course, I learned a strange truth about life: The *difficulties* were actually the doorways to growth and fulfillment. Yet I have spent my life, both before and after becoming a Christian, unconsciously avoiding painful and uncomfortable situations.

Yet, I realized this morning that most of the insights which have been of value to me in relating to other people were distilled from my own difficulties and pain in trying to wrestle with the problems of life. Some of these things—the conflict with loved ones, the blundering mistakes in trying to learn to pray at home—some of these seemed funny when I wrote or told about them in retrospect. But at the time I was *facing* the situations they were difficult, agonizing encounters from which I wanted to run—and often did.

I cannot recall a single person who has been of real help to me in learning to cope with life who has not personally faced some great difficulties or suffering in his own experience, even though he may have seemed profoundly positive and joyful.

The second thought which struck me was that the experience we call "joy" does not usually come from the trouble-free and effortless periods of life. Rather, joy seems to be distilled from a strange mixture of challenge, risk, and hope. And as I have met in groups with other uncertain Christians to share the difficulties in our families, vocations, and relations with other people, the effect has often been one of deep joy and insight into life—even though the difficulties themselves may not have been overcome.

But if this is true, then I should not run from the risk of difficulty and responsibility as I have done so often. I should quit trying to avoid the challenge of hard tasks but instead thank God for them. Because these things seem to provide the main doorways to character and firsthand knowledge about life.*

My restlessness this morning must have been because I did not want to face the difficulty of writing these pages to you. But doing it has brought a great sense of peace about today. And I hope that for the rest of the day I will spend less time running from the tasks and problems that may lead me to life and wholeness.

··+✦❊✦+··

"People then should rejoice in suffering, strange as it sounds, for this is a sign of the availability of energy to transform their characters. Suffering is nature's way of indicating a mistaken attitude or way of behavior, and . . . to the non-egocentric person every moment of suffering is the opportunity for growth."[14]

Rollo May
The Art of Counseling

"Where there is no strife there is decay: 'The mixture which is not shaken decomposes.' "[15]

Heraclitus

---

* I am not saying that one should go out *looking* for personal pain and difficulties. This tendency can be a mental sickness called masochism. It has been my experience however that one will find plenty of problems and pain to face just trying to do God's will in his own life.

FATHER, thank You that Your Holy Spirit seems to use the hours of conflict and suffering which I experience as "teachable moments" in my life. Help me to distill from difficulties a way of living which is whole and gutty and does not sugarcoat reality. Give me the grace not to reject those Christians whose circumstances have been such that they have never personally faced the fear of failure and the frustration of suffering through something difficult. Thank You that Your presence with me in my weakness often brings endurance and hope.

"More than that, we rejoice in our sufferings, knowing that suffering produces endurance, and endurance produces character, and character produces hope, and hope does not disappoint us, because God's love has been poured into our hearts through the Holy Spirit which has been given to us."

Romans 5:3–5.

Commitment: The End of the Trail Intellectually?

For a long time the notion of making a "total commitment to Christ" seemed like a kind of intellectual suicide to me. In some vague way I had gotten the idea that such a commitment would lead to a narrow, fragmented intellectual life made up of "religious" thoughts, books, and conversations on one hand, and "non-religious" ones on the other. I guess my sense of loyalty made me feel that once I "joined" Christ, I could never again question His existence or His way of life. Since I felt that I would be obligated to think "Christian thoughts," I believed that my mind could not roam in new fields and seek new truths with the freedom to examine anything—a freedom which is very important to me.

However, in the act of offering as much of my life as I could at a particular time to as much of Christ as I could grasp at that moment, I began to learn some fascinating things about the intellectual effects of trying to make a serious gift of one's future to God.

I am discovering that in trying to find God's will and the shape of the Christian life I have begun an adventure so great that its total completion will always be ahead. And this has had a unifying effect on my intellectual life that I had not counted on at all. Years ago the Harvard psychologist Gordon Allport pointed out that the striving for a goal beyond one's reach is thought by many psychologists to be the greatest power for unifying the diverse elements in a personality structure.* Certainly this has seemed to be true in many of the developmental stages of my life.

As an adolescent, for instance, the over-riding purpose of playing basketball affected every part of my living: what I ate, what I drank, how much I slept, and how I did my studies. My whole life was ordered by my desire to play basketball well during high school. I did many other things, but having a single dominant incentive gave me a way to establish my priorities and unify my life during a period which could have been very fragmented. As it turned out, the goal of being a great All American player was beyond my reach. But this only made the unifying effect continue as I played. Because, as Allport pointed out, the *achieving* of a goal is often not nearly as unifying as the *pilgrimage in search of it was.* For instance, the Allies were much more unified in *fighting* the Second World War than when we had won it and should *truly* have had unity.

In trying to commit my life to finding and participating in some of the purposes of Christ, as I can determine them, my energies and abilities are gradually being focused and are working together. I have a point of reference for my learning: what does a book or a new experience in a different field have to say about the world and life as Christ presented them? I have an hypothesis which I can test in all areas of thought and

---

* Allport, Gordon, *Pattern and Growth in Personality.*

relationship. And I sometimes experience a freedom to experiment with and challenge old methods and patterns of teaching the Christian message.

But at other times I push away from God and want to be rich or famous. On such days I have two or more different dominant goals. And I gradually begin to feel split and torn in my attempts to focus all my energies on one or the other. Many times I want to be God's person but want more to be a famous writer some day. And I get caught in a real conflict of motives . . . until I begin again and make a primary commitment of my whole future happiness to Christ—*whatever the outcome may be with regard to my other dominant goals.* Often following such a commitment, I find that paradoxically, I am free to work at my secondary purposes more honestly and creatively, because my ultimate happiness does not depend on succeeding there anymore.

It seems that so many young people today are feeling disintegrated in their lives. They appear to be searching for something, a unifying adventure which will bring into a single focus all of their abilities and energies. I guess I am projecting my own experience on them, because that is what I was looking for all my life: an adventure with a meaning and purpose beyond my grasp—an hypothesis with which to integrate all truths. I guess if I were a professor, I would go and tell them what a relief it is to have found such a unifying adventure in the Christian life . . . because it certainly is.

·+◄║▷+·

"The staking of a [overall] goal compels the unity of the personality in that it draws the stream of all spiritual activity into its definite direction."[16]

Alfred Adler
Psychologies of 1930

"Of course education never is complete, and the process of integration extends throughout life; but that is its fundamental purpose—that out of the chaos which we are at birth order may be fashioned, and from being many we may become one."[17]

William Temple
Nature, Man and God

·+·+❊❂❊+·+·

LORD, help me to realize fully the paradoxical freedom that is found through trying to commit all of life to You. Sometimes I am amazed that this commitment has issued in creativity and a freedom to look in all areas for truth, when I had thought it would mean a narrower, restricted intellectual life. Sometimes as I read philosophy and psychology, I am afraid I will find out that You are not real. But I thank You that it is through the strength which comes in this relationship with You that I find the courage to examine even the evidence which might destroy my faith. And for this I am very grateful.

·+·+❊❂❊+·+·

"Jesus then said to the Jews who had believed in him, 'If you continue in my word, you are truly my disciples, and you will know the truth, and the truth will make you free.' "

Jesus Christ
John 8:31,32

Any Old Bush Will Do

A FRIEND, who is a topflight management consultant and a very sharp Christian layman, went to Europe several years ago. He was excited because he had always wanted to visit the Christian shrines in England and on the continent. He went to Aldersgate Street where John Wesley's "heart was strangely warmed," to Wittenberg and to Rome, where Luther's incisive turnings took place. But as he saw these places, which have become shrines for many Protestant Christians, he was frankly disappointed. He had expected to be inspired and awed, but these were just plain buildings and towns.

As he thought about his disappointment, he realized that these had been just ordinary places when the action had taken place which later made them important. In each case the thing that made these churches and cities shrines was that each was a simple setting in which a man had made a decision concerning God's will for himself—a time when someone turned with his whole life, faced God, and chose Him over "things." The *events which followed* were so significant that people now travel for miles just to see the site where the decision was made.

In considering this I realize that so often I have looked for a special place or dramatic circumstances in which I could do God's will. I remembered a sermon another friend once preached about the places where faith can blossom and lives can be committed. He spoke of Moses and the burning bush, and called the sermon, "Any Old Bush Will Do."

The potential shrines in our lives, then, may not be exciting sites or meetings but rather circumstances in which we run out of our own strength and turn to God, offering Him our futures, whatever the cost. The birth of a deeper transforming faith seems to be the event which melds the decision, the deeds, and the place into a shrine. And for this, *any old bush will do*—any old loneliness or frustration, fear, anxiety, or broken relationship—or any of the outward circumstances in which we find ourselves when we commit our lives to Him. Any of these simple "places" where faith comes alive may one day become for us a Christian shrine—any old house, or kitchen sink, or office chair—wherever you are reading this . . . right now.

·⋅+⋅◄❄►+⋅·

IN A GARDEN:

". . . I cast myself down I know not how, under a certain figtree, giving full vent to my tears . . . I sent up these sorrowful words; How long? how long, 'tomorrow, and tomorrow'? Why not now? Why not is there this hour an end to my uncleanness?

"So was I speaking, and weeping in the most bitter contrition of my heart, when, lo! I heard from a neighbouring house a voice, as of a boy or girl, I know not, chanting, and oft repeating, 'Take up and read; Take up and read.' Instantly, my countenance altered, I began to think most intently, whether children were wont in any kind of play to sing such words; nor could I remember ever to have heard the like. So checking the torrent of my tears, I arose; interpreting it to be no other than a command from God, to open the book, and read the first chapter I should find. For I had heard of Antony, that coming in during the reading of the Gospel, he received the admonition, as if what was being read, was spoken to him; *Go, sell all that thou hast, and give to the poor, and thou shalt have treasure in heaven, and come and follow me.* And by such oracle he was forthwith converted unto Thee. Eagerly then I returned to the place where Alypius was sitting; for there had I laid the volume of the Apostle, when I arose thence. I seized, opened, and in silence read that section, on which my eyes first fell: *Not in rioting and drunkenness, not in chambering and wantonness, not in strife and envying: but put ye on the Lord Jesus Christ, and make not provision for the flesh,* in concupiscence. No further would I read; nor needed I: for instantly at the end of this sentence, by a light as it were of serenity infused into my heart, all the darkness of doubt vanished away."[18]

Augustine
The Confessions of St. Augustine

IN AN OFFICE:

LORD, help me to make this chair and this room a shrine in my own pilgrimage by offering myself to You right now. It is frightening to me to call You "Lord" when I realize that means that I am signing up to be Your servant—to go and do and be according to Your designs, even if they should conflict with my own. Although it is easy for me to say "Lord" most days, sometimes—as right now—I realize the awesome and unconditional response for which You are asking. And I want to say with young Augustine, "not yet Lord." At times like this, I realize why there are so few Christian shrines.

··+ ◄◄▮▮►► +··

OR ON A HIGHWAY:

"Thus I journeyed to Damascus with the authority and commission of the chief priests. At midday, O king, I saw on the way a light from heaven, brighter than the sun, shining round me and those who journeyed with me. And when we had all fallen to the ground, I heard a voice saying to me in the Hebrew language, 'Saul, Saul, why do you persecute me? It hurts you to kick against the goads.' And I said, 'Who are you, Lord?' And the Lord said, 'I am Jesus whom you are persecuting. But rise and stand upon your feet; for I have appeared to you for this purpose, to appoint you to serve and bear witness to the things in which you have seen me and to those in which I will appear to you, delivering you from the people and from the Gentiles—to whom I send you to open their eyes, that they may turn from darkness to light and from the power of Satan to God, that they may receive forgiveness of sins and a place among those who are sanctified by faith in me.' "

Acts 26:12–18

"I Love You, Lord, But I Don't Feel Your Presence"

I WAS NERVOUS waiting outside the hotel room for my appointment with Dr. Benton, who was conducting a series of seminars at our church. Finally my turn came.

"I pray regularly," I told him, "but so much of the time I don't feel that God hears me. Not only that, but I don't feel anything much, even when I tell Him I love Him. To pray at times like that seems insincere."

As we talked, I confessed that frequently I didn't feel anything during the communion service either.

The minister leaned back in his chair and thought a minute.

"Are you married?" he asked.

"Yes."

"Do you kiss your wife as you go out the door on the way to work?"

"Yes," I smiled. "Every day."

"Does it give you a great feeling of love every time you kiss her at the doorway?"

I had to admit that sometimes I couldn't even remember whether I had kissed her or not by the time I got to the office.

Dr. Benton identified with my experience, but said that occasionally when he kissed his wife, he was overwhelmed by how much she meant to him as a person. All of those kisses at the door were threads, weaving the fabric of their daily lives into the kind of relationship in which great feelings of love could be experienced naturally and fully when they came. As a Christian, Dr. Benton said that he felt the same way about habits of prayer and worship. Sometimes he did not sense much substance in his feelings for God during his private prayers or at the communion rail, but at other times he was almost overcome by feelings of hope and gratitude to God for His love, acceptance, and for giving him meaning and purpose for his life.

As I was going down the elevator, I could not help smiling when I thought of his analogy about marriage. I remember, when Mary Allen and I were still engaged, arguing with my father about what kind of dog our *children* should have. I recalled the "accidental" touching of our hands in a church pew, and laughing about all of the hamburgers and tuna fish salad we had to eat when we were first married, or even the agony of worrying together about a sick child. And I saw that Dr. Benton was right: a deep loving relationship is woven out of a good many mundane responses which do not *feel* like love at all . . . at the time.

··◄▣►··

". . . this fervour is especially characteristic of beginners, and its drying up should be welcomed as a sign that we are getting beyond the first stages. To try to retain it, or to long for its return in the midst of dryness, is to refuse to grow up. It is to refuse the Cross. By our steady adherence to God when the affections are dried up, and nothing is left but the naked will clinging blindly to Him, the soul is purged of self-regard and trained in pure love."[19]

H. A. Hodges
Unseen Warfare

··+·❋+·

Lord, help me to need You and want You so consciously and continually that I will turn to You regardless of my religious feelings. Help me to be willing to walk into the problems of today representing You . . . even though I must go without the certainty of a bag of pat answers or perhaps even without any feeling of Your being with me. But so often I am afraid to take real risks without the sense of Your presence. I guess I am praying for faith, Lord, so that I can act on the reality of Your love . . . even when I cannot "see" it with my senses.

··+·❋+·

"And what is faith? Faith gives substance to our hopes, and makes us certain of realities we do not see."

Hebrews 11:1 (NEB)

Just As I Am . . . When
I Give Up the Jug?

ONE EVENING several years ago I was taking a young
friend out to dinner. He had just graduated from the
university and was going off to enter the Christian ministry
the next day. John was one of those fine, clean young men
who somehow get through college without scar or blemish
from the world. I found him hard to believe, but he was
evidently sincere. We had eaten in a cafeteria and were
talking about his future when a good-looking young woman
sauntered up to our table in a pair of very short shorts,
sandals, and one of those brief halter type tops. She was
followed by a tiny daughter in a similar outfit. I recognized
the woman as a member of the Sunday school class I taught.
The class was rather large, and I had seen her only as a
member of an audience. A few times I had spoken to her
briefly before or after class, but I had definitely noticed her.

Somehow at the cafeteria, however, she looked very "un-
Sunday schooly." I introduced her to my young friend as a
fellow member of the same Sunday school class, and asked if
she would like to join us. She did, and said at once, "There is
something I've been wanting to talk to you about for months."

"What's that?"

"Paul, I think he was a sex deviate."

My young friend's eyes were protruding slightly in horror, and I sort of wished I had not asked.

"Paul who?" I asked, smiling weakly.

She laughed, "You know who I mean, Paul the Apostle."

So we began to talk about Paul's views concerning women and sex. After about forty minutes it was apparent that Paul was not the problem she wanted to talk about, and I told her so.

Her whole attitude changed. She said almost wistfully, "I really believe you've found hope in your faith, and I would honestly like to make this beginning commitment of my life to Christ . . . but I can't do it."

"Why not?" I asked gently.

"Because I've got a personal problem that I can't seem to resolve." She was biting her lips and looking down at a paper napkin she had folded into a small bulky square.

"But that's why Christianity is called 'good news,' " I said, coming on strong. "We can't solve our own basic hangups and separations, and God is offering through the Holy Spirit to furnish us the motivating power to cope with the seemingly impossible situations in life. That's why I'm such a nut about Christianity. I can't promise to change anything. All I can do is to accept His love and grace."

"But," and she hesitated . . . "I don't feel acceptable until I whip this problem."

"Listen, Susan, the old song doesn't say, 'Just as I am when I whip my major problem.' It says, 'Just as I am without *one plea*,' one *promise*, one *guarantee!*"

She looked at me with the strangest dawning look of hope, "Do you really believe that?" She said.

"I'd bet my life on it."

She looked down at her hands for several minutes. "All

right," she said, almost as a challenge, "I'm committing adultery every Thursday night with a man who has a wife and several young children. And I *cannot* quit. Now can I come into your Christian family?"

I just looked at her. I certainly had not expected that. My first conditioned reaction as a Christian churchman would have been to think she is not ready for Christ, or to say something like, "Baby, don't you think you could at least cut down a little?"

Suddenly I realized how phony we Christians are. Of course we *would* expect her to quit committing adultery. We don't mean "just as I am without one plea." We actually mean, "Just as I am when I *promise* implicitly to straighten up and quit my major sins." And this girl had nailed me with her honesty. She had heard the *real* intent of our church's congregational invitation and knew she did not have the strength to meet its requirements—to quit her "sinning." And yet it was her weakness which had brought her toward Christ in the first place.

I thought about Jesus and what He would have done. Then I looked up at her, "Of course, you can commit your life to Christ just as you are," I smiled. "He knows you want to quit seeing this man, and I don't know where else you can ever *hope* to find the security and strength to break up with him. So if you commit your life to Christ right now, then Thursday night, if you find you can't help meeting your friend, take Christ with you in your conscious mind through the whole evening. Ask Him to give you the desire and the strength to break off the relationship."

And she stepped across the stream and became a Christian.

··◄◄██▌►··

"Sometimes at that moment [in despair] a wave of light breaks into our darkness, and it is as though a voice were saying: 'You are accepted. *You are accepted,* accepted by that which is greater than you . . .'"[20]

Paul Tillich
The Shaking of the Foundations

"There are many religions which know no divine welcome to the sinner until he has ceased to be one. They would first make him righteous, and then bid him welcome to God. But God in Christ first welcomes him, and so makes him penitent and redeems him. The one demands newness of life; the other imparts it. The one demands human righteousness as the price of divine atonement; the other makes atonement in order to evoke righteousness."[21]

J. S. Whale
Christian Doctrine

··+◈+··

THANK YOU, LORD, that the guarantee of strength and integrity in this relationship is Yours and not ours. Thank You that Susan sees this, and wants to change because You have accepted her. Thank You that John was there and that he was able to accept Susan in her weakness. Help me to know that I can *promise* You nothing except my *intention* to be Your person. I pray that You will give me the desire and then the strength to put aside those actions which separate me from You and Your other children. But I am very grateful that Your love does not depend on my success in doing so.

··+◈+··

". . . when the goodness and loving kindness of God our Savior appeared, he saved us, not because of deeds done by us in righteousness, but in virtue of his mercy . . ."

Titus 3:4,5

"The scribes and Pharisees brought a woman who had been caught in adultery. . . . he stood up and said to them, 'Let him who is without sin among you be the first to throw a stone at her.' "

Jesus Christ
John 8:3–7

The Love of a Father

TODAY I CAME out of a "tunnel" into a world that seems bright and filled with hope. I had been having the "blahs" again and had been stumbling through my days with a kind of gray feeling. And this morning I wanted to shout at God, "Where did You go? Where are You?" And then I laughed at my own childishness and thought what a thankless job God has taken on—to love us when so often we are not even conscious of Him.

This started me thinking about the idea that God loves us as a "Father." And I wondered why He does. What would this kind of love be like from His perspective. A scene flashed onto the wall of my memory.

It was in the middle of a winter night some years back, shortly after I had seriously tried to give God the key to my future. One of our children had called out in the darkness, "Daaady!" I was surprised since they usually called their mother. But I got up, stumbled into her room and carried her into the bathroom. The only light was a soft red glow shining on her face from the clay mantles in the gas wall heater. I sat her up on the little pottie seat and bent over to hold her so she wouldn't fall. Her head lolled gently to one side and then she would catch herself, but never quite awaken. As I stood there looking at the softness of her face with her eyes closed, and the slightly tousled long blond hair, I was filled with the most amazing sense of love and gratitude to God for that little girl. I kissed her gently on the nose and thought, "Some day you and I will remember this as a time of great closeness." And I could picture us talking about that night when she was a grown girl. But then I realized that *she* would never remember this midnight closeness—because she had been asleep the whole time I was holding her. But even though she was asleep and would not remember these moments, my own love for her had in some way filled and changed my life as I had quietly helped her though a long winter night.

As I tucked her back in bed with a kiss, it struck me that in some sense this might be one of the reasons the whole Christian venture is worth it to God, in light of our amazing lack of awareness of His presence. I saw that He has been with me all along, loving me and helping me in the most mundane ways, even during those long nights of doubt when I have been spiritually asleep, oblivious to His presence. But even then, when I might least have been trying to respond to Him, His love for me may in some way have warmed His life . . . as my love for my little girl did mine.

···❖···

"Love seeks one thing only: the good of the one loved. It leaves all the other secondary effects to take care of themselves. Love, therefore, is its own reward."[22]

Thomas Merton
No Man Is an Island

···❖···

LORD, thank You that while we were yet sinners, while we were asleep to the fact that You were even interested in us, You loved us enough to die for us in Christ. Help us to be able to love those people in our world who cannot respond to

others because they are still asleep to the meaning of the kind
of love You have given us to pass on.

•∢◆◌▮◌◆▸•

". . . God shows his love for us in that while we were
yet sinners Christ died for us."

Paul
Romans 5:8

"This is my commandment, that you love one another
as I have loved you."

Jesus Christ
John 15:12

To Tell the Truth
(Problem of Integrity No. 2)

"TACT" IS sometimes very difficult for a Christian. We are called on to "speak the truth in love"; and yet I do not believe we are to *worship* being "truthful" in our daily conversations—which truth in any case is often confused with our own *version* of what seems to be true.

Several years ago when I was a new Christian, I decided I would try to be absolutely honest with my wife. We had just moved to a new town and had a good many extra expenses. This transition was making us a little nervous and frantic around the house. In the midst of everything Mary Allen went out and bought a new dress on sale, which she could not return. Buying something new sometimes has a soothing effect on her nerves, and understanding this, I was not too surprised or upset. But when she tried the dress on and asked me how I liked it, I told her I had seen a girl on First Street wearing one just like it that same day. First Street is a very unsavory part of the city. I said the dress was okay, but seeing a cheap-looking girl in one just like it spoiled it for me . . . which was all true. She just glared at me *and never wore the dress.* I was furious. We could not afford it anyway, but to buy the dress and *not wear* it was really terrible.

But I learned something that day. Christian honesty does not mean that I am obligated to express every thought that passes through my mind. I must learn to hear the *real* question someone is asking and answer *that* question, not just the one phrased by the outward words. This was the amazing genius of Jesus' conversation with people. He always saw through their superficial conversation to the real questions they were asking and dealt with them. Mary Allen had been wanting to know, at a deep level, "Am I attractive to you? Is it all right that I impulsively bought this dress just because I feel frantic and dowdy right now? . . . Do you love me?" These were the real "woman questions"; and the true answer to all of them was "yes." But because of my insensitivity, I had answered the superficial question correctly with legalistic honesty—but by so doing I had said "no" to her *real* questions.

Recently I heard a tongue-in-cheek story about a Christian photographer who faced the issue of absolute honesty with his best customer. It seems that an attractive young woman had commissioned him to do an expensive portrait once every ten years. Everything had gone well, but when she was fifty, she was very disappointed with the proofs and more than a little indignant. Charging down to the photographer's studio, she plopped the proofs on his desk. "This picture is not *nearly* as good as the one you made ten years ago!" she said angrily. The photographer looked at the proofs, shook his head thoughtfully for a few seconds, and then nodded sadly, "Well, ma'am, I'm not the man I was ten years ago."

I am not actually suggesting that the photographer did the right thing, but only that he saw the real problem beneath the outward complaint. One might even say that he by-passed the issue. To hear the questions of the heart and answer them is tricky, because of our tendency to avoid the truth when it is painful. But I think this is the risk of trying to move toward the heart of deeper Christian relations. And I believe God wants us to be willing to take risks in trying to love people . . . where they really are.

⁎

". . . I feel the more I know God, that He would sooner we did wrong in loving than never love for fear we should do wrong."[23]

Father Andrew
The Life and Letters of Father Andrew

⁎

LORD, help me not to give people my current medical history when they say, "How are you?" in order to "be honest." Help me to know when they are asking real questions and when they are just saying "hello." Give me a sensitive ear, Lord, to hear the secret needs and doubts behind the façade of words I will walk through today. Give me Your perception, Your radar, to locate the hearts of the people along my way this morning.

⁎

"For he knows the secrets of the heart."

Psalm 44:21

"Knowing their thoughts, he said to them . . ."

Matthew 12:25

The Death and Resurrection
of the Past

NANNIE'S DEAD. Aunt Nannie is dead!" I kept saying it over and over to myself and shaking my head. I couldn't believe it, and yet I knew it was true. I had just seen her body at the funeral home.

I felt sick in the lower part of my stomach—empty. My throat was tight. I wanted to cry but could not because of a lifetime of conditioning to "be a man." But I had not expected such a strong reaction. After all, Mother, Dad, and my only brother had all died or been killed over ten years before. And Nannie was only my aunt.

No, she wasn't "only an aunt." She had lived with us for fifteen years during my grade school and high school years. She had helped spoil me and had given me almost continuous approval (or acceptance when she did not approve) all my life. Now she was gone, and a great sadness had come over me. I knew that whatever good God may have for Christians, Nannie would now have. So I wondered why my grief was so deep. But all I could do was drive around the town which had changed so much, and show the children where she had lived. And I knew something was dying inside me.

That was five months ago, and I finally realized last night why my grief was so deep when Nannie died. I had loved her very much but there was something more. Yesterday we received the initial copy of my first book, *The Taste of New Wine*. I was very excited. I had secretly wanted to write a book since I was a small boy. Mary Allen was excited with me. We didn't think many people would read it, but that did not matter.

I started instinctively for the telephone to call and tell . . . *who?* Then it hit me. Every one who had known me as a child in our home was dead. There was no one to tell who would understand about the dreams and hopes of a little freckle-faced boy who had always tried to look tougher than he was.

When I got in bed that last night, I lay there in the dark and began to weep for the first time in years. A great wave of loneliness came over me. I realized that all the memories of our home had died with Nannie . . . except mine. I was alone with my past. But the flood of grief was a great release.

This morning I can see that last night I stepped across one of the many small streams that separate children from adulthood. And although in one sense I was alone with my past, in another I was not at all—God was with me as a small boy with my hopes and dreams and is with me still. In a sense He and I will always share the memories of the past. In Him not only Nannie but Mother, Dad, and my brother Earle, may in some way that is beyond my understanding still share these memories with me. And in any case I am not alone this morning with my past.

I had never seen before this aspect of Christ's amazing statement, "I am with you alway, even unto the end of the world"—that His presence is really the thread which runs through the memories in a Christian's life, holding the years together, giving them unity of meaning like a string of pearls.

Without His continuing presence with each of us, fear, separation, and death would scatter the Christian family in the wind. And although at times I am still lonely, God's presence and Christ's promises help me not to feel alone when I face my family's death . . . and my own.

··◆❖◆··

" 'The paths of glory lead but to the grave'—whether the 'glory' be the conspicuous achievements (or perhaps only the conspicuousness) of the 'great,' or the modest successes, or the 'quaint deeds' of ordinary men. Not long ago I had occasion to visit a small church in a small town in Virginia where my father was pastor some fifty years ago and where I spent an important part of my boyhood. My father was quiet and modest, a man of remarkable intelligence, humor, and charm and of quite extraordinary goodness, and I found that he was vividly remembered by the oldest members of the church. But the number of these is small and becomes smaller as each.year passes, and quite soon no one at all will remember him. His name will be read for a while—as on a window in the church which they have dedicated to his memory—but the name will mean no more to those who read it than most of the names on the plaques and portraits of old buildings mean to us. Not only will he be silent, as he has been for nearly forty years, but he will no longer speak, for there will be no one to hear him. He will be forgotten. Here is perhaps the supreme pathos of human life—not that we die only but that any real and living memory of us must die too. Unless God is to raise us from death, it is in the end as though we had never been. Our dead have perished leaving no trace except our sad, if grateful, remembrance of them—and in the final reckoning no trace at all.

"Death is the 'last enemy,' and no man, however strong willed and defiant, no matter how stoical or wise,

can wrest the final victory from its hands. Our only hope
is in God. 'Save us, Lord, or we perish'—perish finally
and utterly, along with all we love and treasure."[24]

John Knox
Life in Jesus Christ

LORD, thank You for not only healing the bad memories of
the past through forgiveness but for preserving the good ones
in the memory bank of Your mind. Thank You for Your
awareness of our efforts and strivings, which sometimes seems
to be the only thing that gives meaning when we fail. But
thank You most of all that You have promised to take our
hands when they can no longer reach out to You, and lead us
through the doorway between death and life.

"Lo! I tell you a mystery. We shall not all sleep, but
we shall all be changed, in a moment, in the twinkling of
an eye, at the last trumpet. For the trumpet will sound,
and the dead will be raised imperishable, and we shall
be changed. For this perishable nature must put on the
imperishable, and this mortal nature must put on immortality. When the perishable puts on the imperishable, and the mortal puts on immortality, then shall come
to pass the saying that is written: 'Death is swallowed up
in victory, O death, where is thy victory? O death, where
is thy sting?' The sting of death is sin, and the power of
sin is the law. But thanks be to God, who gives us the
victory through our Lord Jesus Christ."

I Corinthians 15:51–58

It's the Little Things Which Count

WHAT'S SO horrible about leaving the toilet seat up in the middle of the night?" I was furious and defensive. I knew that her reaction at breakfast was far too heavy for the nature of the complaint. That made me mad too . . . and frustrated. It seemed as if everything I did anymore bugged her—innocent mistakes like leaving the shower head at "on" over the bathtub, or forgetting to close the closet door in our bedroom.

I work very hard, spend a lot of time with our family, and try to be generous as a provider. These petty complaints over a few mechanical omissions which were totally accidental, from my perspective, seemed unreasonable, and I was beginning to suspect that I had a nagging wife. But as I drove to work the realization came back that—as bad as it was—the incident the night before was not as big as her anger. (This always means that the present argument is not the real one.) So I began to try to find out the true cause of this rash of getting mad about "little things." It was obvious that something I was doing or being was causing her to run up her red flag.

When the dust settled during the next couple of days, she was able to tell me, "Honey, what these careless things you keep doing *really* say to me is that you don't care enough about me to make an effort to stop doing things which make me mad and frustrated." She stopped and then went on, "I guess I keep waiting for you to remember, and when you don't, I get madder."

"I really *do* care . . ." I started, in defense of myself. But I stopped, because I know that we *do* what we unconsciously want to do in life. I may protest to high heaven that I honestly want to remember things and just cannot. However, I have learned that this is often a deceitful trick the mind plays on itself. Many psychologists have understood that we seldom forget something we *really* want to do unless we have a reason that is hidden . . . often from ourselves.* A golfing enthusiast may forget to take his wife shopping, but he is not likely to forget a golf partner. A young man in love with his girl friend is not apt to forget to pick her up for a date—even if he does forget to do his homework assignment and mow the yard the same weekend. Although I am terribly forgetful about many things, I did not forget a single basketball practice or game during the twenty years I participated in that sport.

Remembering this made me realize that I was evidently not interested in helping Mary Allen's feelings of discomfort and frustration—at least not interested enough to remember certain little common courtesies. Why not, I wondered? I love her and want to be a good husband. And I feel certain that God would have me *at least* care for her needs and comfort with common courtesy.

Then I remembered. Several weeks before I had been feeling especially romantic. And she had been feeling especially tired. I had interpreted her tiredness as a purposeful rejection

---

* Sigmund Freud, *A General Introduction to Psychoanalysis* (New York: Washington Square Press, Inc.), see excellent discussion on the "psychology of errors" in Part I.

and was particularly furious when she claimed later that she had not gotten my signals. I remembered smoldering and thinking, "If she really loved me, she would always be sensitive to my needs!"

So that was my problem. The world was centered in *me* again. But being too proud and "too good a Christian" to set out consciously to punish her for hurting my pride, I repressed the feelings. And I got back at her subtly and unconsciously by forgetting things which hurt her pride—things that made her feel the way I had felt: that she was not loved enough for me to think about her needs and comfort.

And do you know what? When I realized that the problem had started in *me* weeks before and it was that most pervasive sin of self-centeredness, my average improved tremendously in remembering the shower head, the toilet seat, and the closet door.

···✦✦✦···

"For there is only one sin, and it is characteristic of the whole world. It is the self-will which prefers 'my' way to God's—which puts 'me' in the centre where only God is in place. It pervades the universe. It accounts for the cruelty of the jungle, where each animal follows its own appetite, unheeding and unable to heed any general good. It becomes conscious, and thereby tenfold more virulent in man—a veritable Fall indeed."[25]

William Temple
Readings in St. John's Gospel

···✦✦✦···

THANK YOU, GOD, for showing me again that so many of my complaints about other people could be stopped if I could only see my sin. I am amazed at the way I can hide my true motives even from myself. But I am grateful for finding out this morning another of the deceitful maneuvers my ego uses to protect the "fine man" image . . . when a consciousness of my true intentions would destroy it.

·⭒⭓⭒·

"The heart is deceitful above all things, and desperately corrupt; who can understand it? 'I the Lord search the mind and try the heart, to give to every man according to his ways, according to the fruit of his doings.' "

Jeremiah 17:9,10

Squelching a Word of Love

"THAT WAS a great job, Keith!" The man who was speaking is a person whom I deeply respect and love. I had just given a talk in our church, and he was enthusiastically and sincerely affirming me.

"Thanks, but I'm afraid I was too direct," I replied. "I was tired and felt a little hostile." He looked at me strangely, and I went into the educational wing to get ready for church school.

While walking away, I realized what I had done. I had very subtly and unintentionally devalued him as a person. He was trying to tell me that I had done a good job, and he had really meant it. But instead of thanking him for his affirmation, I had told him in effect, "Actually, you aren't really very smart. I heard some negative things about my talk which you didn't hear." Although I had not said that, I saw that my negative reply had in some way rejected him and his kindness in complimenting me in the first place.

Thinking about what had happened, I realized how often I turn people off when they try to say something nice to me. If I happened to make a high score on an examination in college, for instance, and someone said, "Congratulations," I might have laughed and come back with something cute like, "As much time as I spent studying for that one, an orangutan would have done well." I seemed to turn attention away from their attempts to affirm me . . . thinking somehow that I was being humble.

But now I am beginning to see that instead of humility, this inability to accept praise or affirmation is really an insidious form of pride and insecurity. Further, it represents a completely thoughtless attitude toward the needs of the one trying to offer the congratulations. If a person is sincere with his compliments, he is going out on a limb to identify with me. He is reaching out to say, "I, too, feel as you do or appreciate life as you do." Or, "In some sense we are brothers or I would not have responded to what you said." But my reply of supposed humility has turned the attention *away* from him and toward me and my cleverness. I have devalued his love by joking or saying in effect, "No, we are *not* alike, because you misinterpreted my performance." Or, "Your perception is faulty." Or, "If you are like me, you are really a dummy, for any dolt could have done what I have."

It is clear to me now that with all my apparent willingness, as a Christian, to love other people, I fail to love them when I refuse to hear their attempts to love me. I suppose I reject their love because I'm afraid it is unreal, and I cannot risk being hurt—in case they do not mean it—or sometimes I evidently want to appear humble, if they do mean it. So I protect myself from being hurt or from looking proud by dismissing as insignificant any attempts people make to say affirming things to me. Never before had I realized fully the negative, squelching effect of refusing to accept another's kind words.

Since making these discoveries, I am going to try to look people in the eye and say simply and warmly, "Thank you," if they try to say something positive to me. At a deep level I know that anything worthwhile I have is from God. And somehow, by letting people express positive feelings to me through a handshake and a few words, I think something is completed in the attempt to communicate the love of God in human terms.

·+◄░▶+·

"Words and magic were in the beginning one and the same thing, and even today words retain much of their magical power. By words one of us can give to another the greatest happiness or bring about utter despair . . . Words call forth emotions and are universally the means by which we influence our fellow creatures. Therefore let us not despise the use of words. . . ."[26]

> Sigmund Freud
> *A General Introduction to*
> *Psychoanalysis*

·+◄░▶+·

THANK YOU, GOD, that You are willing to receive my stumbling and often half-sincere attempts to praise You. Since You showed us in Christ that it is important for us to be able to receive, please give us the grace we need to do so. I am grateful that You take these praises of mine seriously rather than rejecting me with a denial or a joke, which would leave me alone and sorry I tried. Help me to learn how to love. But O Lord, give me the security to risk *receiving* from other people . . . love, which I fear may not be real.

·+◄░▶+·

IT IS HARD TO RECEIVE:

"Peter said to him, 'You shall never wash my feet.' Jesus answered him, 'If I do not wash you, you have no part in me.' Simon Peter said to him, 'Lord, not my feet only but also my hands and my head!' "

> John 13:8,9

A Widow's "Might"

THIS WEEK in a small group we were talking about how we might find a place of lasting importance in our community in which to participate in God's work. We began by examining those things we were presently doing which involved helping people outside of our own families. Some of the usual church and civic activities were mentioned. Then we came to a perky, bright little white-haired lady named Jane who is eighty years old. She had been a registered nurse all her adult life, and we had all been affected by her frankness, vitality, and her love of God.

Jane said, "I've found that there is a terrible problem among the bedridden old people in this town. Many of them suffer constantly because they are constipated, and there is no one to give them the proper nursing care of an enema." And so this dear, cheery little saint has been going around among the poor giving the very sick old men and women in our town a fantastic number of enemas for Christ's sake.

We were embarrassed and tried not to smile when she first began to talk; but as she continued, I quit being embarrassed and started hearing what this remarkable woman was saying to us. I drew her out and asked her how she had started nursing people in her spare time for no charge.

She thought a minute and then smiled, as she remembered. "When I was a red-haired young nurse," she began, "I got very upset at the hospital in which I was working. They would turn poor people away who could not show evidence of financial capability. This bothered me a lot because some of them had no place to go." It was apparent that she had been very angry. Jane went on to tell us how she had prayed about what to do. As a result she had opened her small home to some of the destitute sick women, finally filling it with cots and beds. Some of her patients were Catholics, some were Protestants, and others were non-Christians. They had all sorts of different cultural and social backgrounds, but all were sick. She nursed them when she got off work.

Not having much money, Jane soon spent all she had. One morning she sat down on the front step and cried into a $30.00 milk bill, which she had no way of paying. Having told God that she could not put these sick people out in the street, she had no idea where to go for help. She suddenly remembered a fiery young Episcopal priest (who was to become one of the outstanding bishops in the church). Putting on her coat she rushed to his office. She was very frightened—afraid he would not even listen. But she got in and told him her story—how in obedience to that which she felt God had revealed to her in her prayer, she had opened her house to all kinds of sick people. And she had spent everything on their care.

The big priest looked at her with a twinkle in his eye, and said with mock seriousness, "Why have you got all these Baptists and Methodists and Catholics? Maybe you shouldn't be in the Episcopal Church."

"I am *not* leaving my church!" she said with tears coming to her eyes. "And *you* should help me!"

"What in the world do you want me to do?" he asked with a questioning gesture.

Jane had no idea how much to ask for, so she plopped the unpaid milk bill into his hand, and said, "Well, you can begin by paying the milk bill." And he did.

Years later, that bishop completed an amazing career of service and influence. Most people never knew that the mammoth Christian medical center he had promoted—for Baptists, Methodists, and *all* kinds of people—might never have been built except for the vision he had seen in the simple obedience of a poor little red-headed nurse . . . who was trying to love her Lord and the people around her.

·•✦✦✦✦•·

". . . The really important thing is that in those early days the pagans saw in Christianity and in the Church a power that could cope with and mend the human situation. They saw in Christianity a power which they did not possess—and they wanted it. It will always be true that the outsider will have no use for an alleged faith which is demonstrably ineffective. Long ago Nietzschze, the atheist philosopher, issued the challenge: 'Show me that you are redeemed and then I will believe in your Redeemer.' The greatest converting influence of all is a life which clearly and obviously is possessed of a power which can cope with the human situation in all its problems, in all its tragedy, and in all its pain."[27]

William Barclay
Turning to God

·•✦✦✦✦•·

Lord, I am glad that You made a moving drama of the Christian life instead of a study course in abstract philosophy. Thank You that the role You have given me is important to You as the Author—however insignificant I may feel as I look at the "great ones" in the world's eyes. I am grateful that the "size" of our outward results does not seem as important to You as the depth of the commitment our behavior reveals. Help me to "commit it all" today.

·⁺⦅⦆⁺·

"And he sat down opposite the treasury, and watched the multitude putting money into the treasury. Many rich people put in large sums. And a poor widow came, and put in two copper coins, which make a penny. And he called his disciples to him, and said to them, 'Truly, I say to you, this poor widow has put in more than all those who are contributing to the treasury. For they all contributed out of their abundance; but she out of her poverty has put in everything she had, her whole living.' "

Jesus Christ
Mark 12:41–44

Mixed Motives—A Problem
for the Intense
(Problems of Integrity No. 3)

MOMMY, I'M not sure if I am being nice to these people because I like them or because I believe it will make them think I'm a neat kid. And it worries me. Should I quit being so friendly?"

The lady who was showing me this passage from a letter was puzzled. It was from her young teenage daughter who was away at camp for the summer. The mother said that she had not worried about such things when she was a girl and asked me what I thought about the letter.

Smiling a little to myself, I realized that I could have written a similar letter at many different times in my life. The problem—of mixed motives—has given me fits in several different ways. Those of us who have a deep need to be accepted, and for whom acceptance as a child was subtly contingent on our "being good," may have more trouble with motivational nit-picking than other people. Sometimes in school, I remember worrying about whether I was thoughtful to other kids because I meant it or because by being friendly to them I would likely be elected to class offices. Although I

95

knew at some level that both motives were there and that both were pretty natural, I wanted to be *sure my* motives were right—like the little girl in the letter.

When I became a Christian, this occasional compulsive need to have pure motives took an especially insidious form, which brought the whole business to a head. Beginning to witness in other churches as a layman, I wondered sometimes if I were going because I wanted to tell people about God . . . or about me. This worried me, since I really wanted to be God's person and to do His will. On one occasion I almost called a minister and canceled a meeting because I wasn't sure if I were going for God or for Keith. But having put off contacting him until it was very late, I went ahead and drove to the church—knowing that my motives were definitely mixed. Before I spoke that night, I prayed silently that God would use me "if You can use a man as full of himself as I am." After I started speaking, I forgot all about my motives.

Several days later a man who attended the meeting came to my office. He said that he had been desperate and had almost lost hope, but as a result of attending the session that night had decided to give life another try. After he left, I sat thinking about what had happened.

In the first place, my desire to keep my motives spotless and pure had almost kept me from helping a man who was really desperate. I saw how totally self-centered this "keeping myself righteous" is. It constitutes a strange kind of Christian idolatry—I was worshiping clean motives. Keeping them spotless was more important somehow than going ahead with mixed motives and letting God possibly help someone through me.

In the second place, it came crashing home to me that my motives are *always* mixed to some degree—and that most likely they always will be in this life. So that for me, the leap of faith in witnessing for Christ is to go, knowing my needs for attention, but taking the risk that I will speak for Him instead of for myself. I must go in faith, praying that God will use me in spite of my self-centeredness.

In fact, after all these years, I simply pray that God will free me to point over my shoulder to Him. Because when it comes right down to it, all I have to tell about is what I have seen and heard of Him—how He is helping me to find freedom, occasionally to love other people, and even to accept myself with my mixed motives.

··+◆◉◆+··

"What can we take with us on this journey to we do not know where? What we must take is the knowledge of our own unending ambiguous motives. . . .

"The voice that we hear over our shoulders never says, 'First be sure that your motives are pure and selfless and then follow me.' If it did, then we could none of us follow. So when later the voice says, 'Take up your cross and follow me,' at least part of what is meant by 'cross' is our realization that we are seldom any less than nine parts fake. Yet our feet can insist on answering him anyway, and on we go, step after step, mile after mile. How far? How far?"[28]

Frederick Buechner
The Magnificent Defeat

··+◆◉◆+··

DEAR LORD, help me not to be a Christian Pharisee who is more interested in being ethical than in loving You and Your people. Be with the little girl who wrote the letter to her mother, and help her to understand that sometimes she will have to risk her motives in order to do anything good. Give us both the courage to follow You even if it means taking the risk, as You did, of being misunderstood. I want to resist phoniness . . . yet without wallowing in the problems of mo-

tivation. It all seems very complex, and sometimes I do not
even understand my behavior after the fact. So I am offering
myself and my subtly mixed motives to You, asking that You
will take me beyond such self-centered preoccupations into
Your loving perspective.

··⁺◄❀►⁺··

"I do not understand my own actions. For I do not do
what I want, but I do the very thing I hate . . .
Wretched man that I am! Who will deliver me from this
body of death? Thanks be to God through Jesus Christ
our Lord! . . ."

Romans 7:15,24,25

Motivation for Christian Education: A Changed Life

H OW CAN a church leader motivate people even to come out to *hear* the gospel, much less to become Christians?" This question seems to be implicit in every leadership meeting I attend. I have found a single recurring answer echoing down the years. For many people there is only one universally effective way to interest people in Christianity—and that is to expose them to a person with whom they can identify, a person who is finding hope and meaning in Christ in his own life. For years I was a little hesitant about the idea of new Christians trying to influence other people before they really understood some of the implications of the gospel. However, not long ago something happened that made me rethink this whole matter.

While on a speaking trip in another state, I was restless and tired. Feeling phony and miserable, I did not want to speak to this particular group. How could I possibly project hope and purpose concerning the Christian life?

Waiting my turn to speak, I looked out over those hundreds of strange faces. I wondered if anyone else had come to this meeting unwillingly . . . and could not shake loose from the slough of self-pity and the frustration of not being able to control his circumstances. But after I had finished speaking, I found myself still standing before the lectern, sort of hesitating. Finally, I heard myself saying something I had never said before—and was a little embarrassed because it sounded like some kind of gimmick: "You know, I have the strangest feeling that I came all this way to talk to one of you who may be going through some of the same feelings of frustration and self-pity I am. And if you think you are the person, I would like to meet you after this session."

As I sat down, I mentally kicked myself in the backside. "Why did you say a stupid thing like that? These people will think you are some kind of a kook." But it was too late.

After the program a large number of men came to extend the courtesy of greeting the speakers. As the line came by, I forgot all about my closing remarks until a short, heavy-set man with glasses and black wavy hair walked up to me. When he shook my hand, he gripped it with great intensity. I looked into his eyes and saw a couple of tears start down his cheeks. Leaning forward, I said quietly, "Say, if you have a minute I'd like to talk to you." He nodded. I pointed over to a corner and said I would be there in a few minutes.

As soon as I could break loose, I went to him. "What are you doing here?" I asked him.

"This is the damnedest thing that ever happened to me. I am an attorney and travel a lot. Although we belong to this denomination," and he nodded toward the group still clustered around the speaker's platform, "it hasn't really meant anything to me in years. I certainly never planned to come to this meeting. As a matter of fact . . ." and here he stopped and looked at me a little uneasily. But then he went on, "As a matter of fact, I have a mistress in this town and was coming to see her—though I was supposedly on a business trip. For weeks I have been feeling very guilty. I wanted out of this relationship, but couldn't seem to break it off. Well, anyway, when I got out of my car a block from this church in front of her apartment, who should come charging up to clap me on the back but three guys from my home church. I almost fainted as one of them asked, 'What are you doing here, Joe?' 'I, uh . . . I'm just passing through,' I lied, scared to death they were going to see the guilt written all over me.

" 'Hey, great. We're just going down to hear some Christian businessmen speak. You've gotta come with us.' And I was afraid to say no for fear I'd somehow give myself away.

"But as I sat there in the meeting and heard you speak about a new start in life—a life with purpose and meaning, I was amazed. I had given up on having any purpose and meaning and had been filled with self-pity. I had no idea what to do. Then you stood up there and looked squarely at me and said what you did, and I knew that I was the one." He stopped talking and looked at me.

"Listen," I said, not really knowing what to do since I had to catch a plane. "We haven't much time. Would you like to commit your whole future to God, including the relationship with this woman?"

He just stood there biting his lips, and finally said, "Boy, I *sure would!*"

"All right. There are a couple of things involved in beginning, as I understand it. One is to confess that you really want your own way more than God's; and if you can do that, then ask God, as He is revealed in Christ, to come into your own inner life and show you how to live for Him . . . and then give Him permission to make you want to."

In a prayer, standing in the corner of that huge church, Joe made a new beginning. I pointed out that Christianity was not a "ticket to heaven" but a way of life that starts now and transcends death, and that all he had done with me was to make a bare beginning—now he had to begin to learn to live again.

I heard my name called and noticed that the people who were to drive me to the airport were looking at their watches. Hating to leave this man, I said, "Hey, listen, Joe, I'll make a deal with you. I'll pray for you every morning for a month if you will pray for me. If you want to go on after that, write me a card and say, 'You're on for another month,' and I'll stay with you a month at a time from now on."

Joe was in tears as he shook my hand. I hated to leave but had to. Glancing at my watch, I saw that the whole interview had lasted about twelve minutes.

When I got home from that trip at the end of the month, there was a letter from Joe. He had begun to live for God. Things looked great. He had started by breaking off the relationship with his mistress. Already it was hard, but he was going to try for another month if I would stick with him.

Well, I knew old Joe was in for some real adjustments. And as the months went by, I was amazed at the way God was getting hold of this man. He began reading the Scriptures and all the books he could get his hands on about living the Christian life, and he began going to his church and having long talks with his minister. Joe began to see his self-centeredness and changed his behavior toward his family and friends in the little southwestern town of a few thousand in which he lived. During all this time I had not seen Joe or talked to him. All he knew was that someone he had met one day was praying for him at 6:30 every morning.

About a year later Joe wrote and said he had told a few people about what was happening to him, but he did not feel they understood him. If I would come to his church, he said he would get these people together for a discussion about living for Christ as a businessman.

This was a very busy time in my life. But I had gotten Joe into this, and the circumstances were so unusual that I thought the least I could do would be to go and visit with the little group to which he was trying to witness. So I went.

I got in just in time for the meeting. Joe met my plane and was very excited as we drove to his church. He said he was sure glad I was there, because several people in town had come right out and asked him what had happened to his life. Since I had never written any books or articles, his friends would know me only as "a friend of Joe's." As we arrived at the church, the minister said that he was glad I'd come and that Joe had really helped him personally. By this time we were a few minutes late. We went through a door at one end of the church to meet the friends who were curious about Joe's life. I stopped for several seconds . . . looking into the faces of over 800 people crowded into every corner and aisle of that church and adjoining rooms.

I realized in that moment that all of the promoted programs and Christian education plans in the world will be virtually worthless to motivate people to become Christians —unless they see some ordinary person like Joe who is finding hope and a new way to live in Christ. And then they will listen.

··+ ✦❈❈✦ +··

"The most pragmatic of reasons for seeing that Christ is the most dependable of realities is that of changed human lives. When we consider Saul of Tarsus on the road to Damascus, we are in the realm of the empirical as contrasted with the merely speculative. Saul said it was the Living Christ who had met him, and the person who seeks to deny this is confronted with the fact of a permanent change in Saul's character. We cannot, of course, know whether a man is lying when he says 'I believe,' because belief is intrinsically internal and personal, but the evidence of changed lives is something which other people can observe. In Saul's case the change was so radical that it led to the production of some of the finest literature of the world, a literature which would not have been produced apart from the crucial encounter.

"The evidence of lives changed by contact with Christ is so abundant that the full story can never be told; it is, indeed, of a kind not matched anywhere in any culture. The changed lives have come about, not primarily by a set of ideas or by acceptance of a doctrine, but by commitment to a Person."[29]

D. Elton Trueblood
A Place to Stand

LORD, we have somehow lost the art of living in our attempts to educate people into the Kingdom of God. Sometimes I have reduced Your Way into a study program "about" the faith of the church. At other times I have tried the emotional techniques of psychology and industry to motivate people to participate in the life of Your church. Help me, Lord, to spend time with persons, time in which we can discover together how to live our days and nights for You. Help me to learn again the amazing motivating power of lives which are in the process of discovery and change. Give me something of the patience and vision You had in spending two-thirds of your ministry with a group of twelve.

"And as he [Jesus] was getting into the boat, the man who had been possessed with demons begged him that he might be with him. But he refused, and said to him, 'Go home to your friends, and tell them how much the Lord has done for you, and how he has had mercy on you.' And he went away and began to proclaim in the Decapolis how much Jesus had done for him; and all men marveled."

Mark 5:18–20

The Servant

LAST WEEK I was very busy trying to get what seemed like a thousand things done before leaving for a three-day speaking trip on the East Coast. There hadn't been time to prepare my talks so I was under a lot of pressure when a friend, a fine Christian woman, called. A couple she knew was having marital problems. "They might call you," she said, "because they could not agree on either a minister or a psychiatrist." But my friend thought it crucial that I see them if at all possible.

It seems that the majority of the people I've counseled with lately have had marital problems. Even though I was dead tired, I agreed to talk with them, hoping they wouldn't call. But sure enough at almost midnight the telephone rang. The man called me "Reverend" Miller (in what I thought was a condescending tone).

"Keith Miller," I said with some definiteness. "I am a layman."

"I'd like to make an appointment to see you," he said without any details or preliminary remarks. Just when I started to ask who was calling, it occurred to me that he must be the husband of the couple having troubles. He proceeded to set up the appointment. I was too tired and off balance to say, "Wait just a minute, friend." Besides I realized the man was under pressure and had probably put off calling all evening. So the appointment was made for one o'clock the following day at our house.

I was irritated since this meant driving five miles from my writing hideout in the middle of the day. Asking myself, "What kind of a Christian are you if you can't help another human being in trouble?" helped some. But it made me mad that this guy was treating me like some sort of a hired hand. I was only seeing him as a friend, with no intention of charging him as a counselor. So I prayed to be open to the man, and I was (at least consciously) by the time I got home the next day at 12:30. The telephone rang at 1:10 and the man said, "Something has come up and I won't be able to make it to your house." I started to tell him he could just forget it, but then it occurred to me that he might be avoiding the conference purposely. And from what my friend had said, this man could be in serious trouble. So I agreed to see him the following day.

We had a good visit, but it was apparent that their marital problems were severe. By that time my schedule was really pressing. Not long after the husband left, his wife called and after a long conversation, she asked for an appointment. Knowing how hard it is to wait when things seem to be closing in on you, I agreed to see her at 11:00 the following morning.

I rushed home at 10:55 to find that the woman had just called and left word: something had come up and she was not going to be able to come. I was *furious!* Three days had been fouled up by these people. They didn't even have the courtesy to consider how much inconvenience I was going through for them. I wanted to call and tell them that one of their problems was "self-centeredness." And further I wanted to inform them that I was very busy myself . . . and then it hit me: how important I must think I am if a thing like this can make me as mad as it did. Here were two people in the agony of struggling to keep their home together—with no telling what other complications—and I was incensed that they were treating me like a common servant . . . when that is what I have committed my life to be: a servant to Christ and His suffering people. But my behavior told me that secretly I must want to be treated like a big shot writer and counselor.

·+◄⧉▷+·

"For the self-flattery of our nature is very subtle and few can discern it. Secretly it pursues only its own ends, though meanwhile its outward conduct is such, that it seems to us we have but the single aim of pleasing God, though in actual fact this is not so . . . So if a man does not watch himself well, he may begin some activity with the sole purpose of pleasing the Lord, but later, little by little, introduce into it a self-interest, which makes him find in it also a satisfaction of his own desires, and this to such an extent that the will of God becomes completely forgotten."[30]

Lorenzo Scupoli
Unseen Warfare

"In renunciation it is not the comforts, luxuries and pleasures that are hard to give up. Many could forego heavy meals, a full wardrobe, a fine house, et cetera; it is the ego that they cannot forego. The self that is wrapped, suffocated in material things—which include social position, popularity, and power—is the only self they know and they will not abandon it for an illusory new self . . . which they may never attain."[31]

Mahatma Gandhi
*Ghandi, His Life and Message
for the World*

·+◄⧉▷+·

FORGIVE ME, LORD, and help me not to look for the respect and acclaim of people but to be willing to die to my self-concern enough to accept them just as they are. For the good of this couple I do not think I should be a doormat, and I will be firm in any future contact with them with regard to their keeping appointments if they want help. But I see that the worst problem is mine—not theirs. Change my attitude, Lord, to one of a servant.

···✦✥❃✥✦···

"And Jesus called them to him and said to them, 'You know that those who are supposed to rule over the Gentiles lord it over them, and their great men exercise authority over them. But it shall not be so among you; but whoever would be first among you must be your servant, and whoever would be first among you must be slave of all. For the Son of man also came not to be served but to serve, and to give his life as a ransom for many.' "

Jesus Christ
Mark 10:42–45

Temptation: A Strong Wind
for a Flickering Flame

TEMPTATION IS a strange experience for me. I want to be God's person. But I also have some deep human needs for approval, affection, and the satisfaction of strong physical and emotional drives. When wrestling with a specific temptation, I seem to change into a different person inside. I have a kind of channel vision and only see the object of my resentment, greed, or lust. All else is blotted out. I am no longer the smiling, friendly Christian, but instead am an intense and sweating stranger—yet not a stranger, for I know this one so well. Reason waits outside the door of temptation for me. I argue against my conscience and dazzle myself with agile rationalizations. By that time the battle is usually lost.*

Of course, sometimes there are long periods of peace and productivity when all the dragons appear to be dead. But then, one day when I am seemingly in good control of my emotions, I am suddenly in the midst of temptation. My

---

* Thomas à Kempis pointed out in the *Imitation of Christ* that the only time to stop temptation is at the first point of recognition. If one begins to argue and engage in a hand to hand combat, temptation almost always wins the day.

senses are alive to the object of my resentment or my desire. I am practically engulfed in the urge to surrender to my inclination—to glorify my desires above everything—the instant they are born. And sweeping away reason, goodness, God's will, caution, and potential guilt—I succumb.

People who have not had this experience as Christians would make poor counselors for men like me. I know you may say that I am weak. And of course that is the truth. I am weak. But my question is, "What does a weak, yet sincerely committed, Christian do when temptation gets through his blockers and tackles him with a crippling jolt?"

My reactions have been varied. Almost always I feel inadequate and do not like myself. I shy away from prayer, feeling that somehow I could have resisted longer and not succumbed. It is strange, but because of my pride, I always think I could have conquered. But this notion rests on the dubious idea that if I am truly committed to Christ, I *can* control all my actions with reason and determination—if I will just try hard enough.

The truth about the Christian life seems to be, however, that *no one* bats a thousand in facing temptation. As a matter of fact, most of the saints felt that their averages were pretty low. We can improve our performance, and I thank God that this is so. But evidently in this life we will always have the occasional experience of succumbing to temptation. The sad truth is that much of the time I am too weak to resist, and my failure is simply a hard cold fact with which I must live. I have to come to God with the horribly uncomfortable feeling of failure. And finally, with no excuses, I force myself to my knees before Him in confession, asking for restoration to a state of usefulness and self-acceptance by His grace.

I thank Him that this process is what the gospel is all about —the forgiveness of the glorification of our desires and pride to a position above everything, including Him. And asking Him for a new set of controlling desires, I thank Him for the miracle of forgiveness and the strange new start He can give me. I pull myself to my feet, brush the caked spiritual mud from my clothes and walk into another day as His child.

⁕⁕⁕

"First don't dwell on yourself, do not say: 'How could I be such as to allow and suffer it?' This is a cry of proud self-opinion. Humble yourself and, raising your eyes to the Lord say and feel: 'What else could be expected of me, O Lord, weak and faulty as I am.' "[32]

Lorenzo Scupoli
Unseen Warfare

"I resolve to meet evil courageously, but when even a small temptation cometh, I am in sore straits. That which seemeth trifling sometimes giveth rise to a grievous temptation; and when I think myself to be secure, and least expect it, I am overcome by a light breath."[33]

Thomas à Kempis
The Imitation of Christ

⁕⁕⁕

DEAR LORD, I know it must have broken Your heart to realize that even those of us who follow You would get carried away and crush the people around us, trying to satisfy our hungers for attention and power.

Help me not to kid myself about my real needs and desires and cloak them with phony righteous motives or plead "weakness" as an excuse for succumbing to temptation. I realize that I am capable of almost any sin. Give me the courage to face You more realistically. I pray that You will make those things which are creative, beautiful, and constructive so attractive to me that I will run toward them . . . away from the crippling world of inordinate self-indulgence.

And Lord, thank you for indicating that You believe a man should be forgiven more than once.

··•◄◙►•··

"Then Peter came up and said to him, 'Lord, how often shall my brother sin against me, and I forgive him? As many as seven times?' Jesus said to him, 'I do not say to you seven times, but seventy times seven.'"

Matthew 18:21,22

The Need to Be Included

THIS WEEK two people have called to ask us for details about a party which is being given by some good friends of ours. In each case we laughed and said that we were sorry we couldn't help them because we were not invited. They were very embarrassed, and we thought the whole thing was funny. In any case, we had another regular commitment to a group of Christians on that night and could not have accepted.

But then, when I was alone in my office, I found myself wondering why they did not invite us, since both couples who called fit our "category" for invitations. And one was not particularly close to the host couple at all. I felt all this even though I realized our friends knew about our other commitment. The insecurities of my childhood came scampering back across the years to make me miserable.

How strange this experience is. I wouldn't trade our Christian life and friends and the meaning we are finding together in Christ for any other way of living we have known—especially the driving, party-filled life. And yet when the first "sounds of the music" reach my ears across the night, I am sometimes gripped by my "inner child of the past" who tells me I am being left out of life. And I realize that it is this built-in incompleteness which keeps me from congratulating myself about my self-sufficiency in Christ, and makes me turn again to God as a child.

In counseling during the past few years, and in my own experience, I have come to see how universal and exaggerated the need to be accepted can be. The desire can be strongly activated even when one is not particularly interested in the event in question.

Some years ago when our children were much younger, we all had been out on a family picnic. When we came home, we were very tired. One of the little girls ran in and asked me to unbutton her dress. I tickled her between each button, a ritual which had delighted her since she was very tiny, and she ran off into her room laughing.

A few minutes later when I went in to kiss the girls good night, our eight-year-old was very long-faced and quiet. She looked up.

"Play with *me*, Daddy."

"Oh no," I told her gently, "it's too late, baby."

"You played with sister," she whispered almost weeping.

"No, I didn't, honey, I just unbuttoned her dress."

"But . . . (and now there were tears in her eyes) . . . but, Daddy, I heard her *laughing*."

This morning here in my office I am remembering that little scene, and I realize that although I can outgrow my concern about not being in the mainstream of certain kinds of "parties and games," I will always have the deep need to be included. And this need will drive me out of myself as a solitary Christian and back to God and His people.

·+◄◈►+·

"Someone has imagined God first fashioning man, and one of the host of heaven, watching, exclaiming in alarm, but you are giving this creature freedom! He will never be wise enough or strong enough to handle it. He will think himself a god. He will boast in his own self-sufficiency. How can you gamble that he will ever return to you? And God replies, I have left him unfinished within. I have left in him deep needs that only I can satisfy, that out of his desire, his homesickness of soul, he will remember to turn to me."[34]

F. B. Speakman
The Salty Tang

LORD, thank You that You have called us Christians into a family and not to a lonely way. Thank You that the longing to be included, which seems to be planted in us from the beginning, has finally been met in a relationship with You and Your people. And thank You for the reminder from the past this morning. As I try to witness to that which I have seen and heard of You today, help me to be more aware of other people who come into Your Christian family at church and of their need to *feel* included . . . when they hear laughter across a room, or a city.

"What we have seen and heard we declare to you, so that you and we together may share in a common life, that life which we share with the Father and his Son Jesus Christ. And we write this in order that the joy of us all may be complete."

I John 1:3,4 (NEB)

Witnessing for the Witness' Sake

THIS MORNING I realized that two very different men had talked to me this week about a common "problem" into which public witnessing has gotten them. One man, named Rick, is very successful materially and has been rather aloof from the average person in his home city for years. Upon making a beginning commitment of his whole life to Christ, he did not like his attitude toward people. But he had not been able to do anything about it.

Being a very talented communicator, Rick was soon asked to speak to groups of laymen concerning his new outlook toward God and people. This past weekend he spoke to 1200 in one meeting. Yesterday he called and laughed, "You crazy fanatics have ruined my whole life style," he said. "Now that so many people know me by sight *as a Christian,* I feel like a 'specimen.' I can't feel easy sneering in traffic snarls anymore. I'm afraid they might be some of the ones who heard me say I'm praying to be more loving. God has finally gotten it across to me through this public speaking, that I really want to be open to people."

The other man, who also made a new beginning with Christ several months ago, is an articulate speaker, too, and has

117

been invited to witness concerning his faith in a widening geographical circle. But the problem which has plagued this man has been adultery. He came to God in Christ, "just as he was," helpless. And he felt accepted. But although he had prayed a lot about it, one problem he still had trouble with was an occasional slip with a woman. For some of you this may sound strange, but the man had made a deep commitment to Christ; and it had changed almost every area in his life. He just had a lingering problem with women, about which he had been praying earnestly.

But as he sat across my desk this week, he looked sort of confused. "You know, Keith, this witnessing is answering my own prayers by ruining my outside sex life." He smiled with a slightly guilty look as he continued, "I thought I really wanted to give up other women for God, but I would find myself compulsively going to my old haunts 'just to see' if God had healed me. And I'd get in bed every time. But this week, a couple of days after I witnessed at that big meeting, I got in my car to take a drive. When I got to the bar, a girl came over and said, 'Say, I heard you speak the other night at that big meeting. What you said was great!' " My friend went on to tell me that the girl had assumed he was through with his former adulterous habits. So he responded to her assumption and went home.

Now *I* smiled. "You'd better be careful what you pray for, Joe. The Lord works in strange ways."

He looked at me and grinned like a small boy. "If I keep up this witnessing business, I'm going to have to go a thousand miles from home to find a *chance* to get in trouble." And we both knew he had somehow rounded a corner with his problem.

In thinking about these two men and their experiences, I thought, "They really missed the point. We're supposed to change our behavior because we *want* to in order to align our lives with God's purposes as we can discover them." But I saw how unreal I was being. These men are very intelligent. Both had already known how they wanted to behave for Christ's sake, yet neither had had the motivational strength to break their well-established habit patterns. But in standing up and identifying with Christ and His loving way of living, they each became *acutely conscious* of different ways in which their integrity was being compromised by un-Christian behavior they had previously been able to "set aside" from this central commitment to God. And while this was happening unseen and inside their lives, audiences were marveling at the witness of that which God had already done for them.

Because of this experience, I realized the value, and almost the necessity, of publicly identifying with Christ's way of life in order to trigger the conscious interruption of some conditioned response patterns of a lifetime. Of course, the changes came because their strength was in God as they were trying to follow His way.

But at the same time I knew that if the changes were made only because of "audiences," the new behavior might be merely a shallow Christian conformity which could dissolve with a simple change in environment. The only conscious changes which have lasted in my life have been those I have made because I felt the old behavior really interfered with my relationship to God.

·+·+◆◈◆+·+·

"We become fully conscious only of what we are able to express to someone else. We may already have had a certain inner intuition about it, but it must remain vague so long as it is unformulated."[35]

Paul Tournier
The Meaning of Persons

BUT THERE IS A DANGER:

"The eyes of people around us exert a great pressure on our designs. These witnesses force us not to give expression to the evil which arises in the heart; we refrain from evil—and our behavior appears correct. Were it not for them our behavior would look quite different; and it often becomes such as long as we are sure that no other eyes can see us. It happens with some people, that as soon as their outer conditions change and they can live more freely, all that was previously concealed, for fear of being seen by others, bursts out and a formerly well-behaved man becomes a drunkard, a debauchee, or even a robber. All these bad impulses were not born at this moment; they existed before, but were denied expression, whereas now they are given free rein and so become manifest."[36]

Lorenzo Scupoli
Unseen Warfare

LORD, thank You that the process of witnessing and writing books about the Life You have made available to us through Christ has helped *me* to remember that I honestly do want to be Your person. I am amazed that I can "forget"; and yet my behavior tells me, again and again, that I have. So Lord, I pray that You will use my attempts at witnessing to teach me if no one else and make me a healthy loving person whose strength is in You.

"Blessed are the men whose strength is in thee, in whose heart are the highways to Zion. . . . They go from strength to strength; the God of gods will be seen in Zion."

Psalm 84:5,7

The Short Unusual Witness of Bennie Abernathy

THIS MORNING I was thinking of how little we know about communication. I tried to imagine the live television pictures from the moon hitting my brain with pinpoint accuracy after traveling untold thousands of miles through the fantastic speeds of the earth's and moon's orbits and their joint travel around the sun. This kind of communication is more than my father could have even imagined. As a matter of fact, I remember seeing a demonstration with him of the first live television equipment when I was a child. I overheard people saying that it was interesting but would never be feasible, because it could only transmit a stationary picture for a few feet.

Just now I thought about the intimate experience I am having as I communicate with you through this book in your mind, perhaps across thousands of miles . . . conceivably over years of time. And yet, even if I am dead when you read this, my living mind is meeting yours, and we are sharing to some degree the communication I am experiencing as I write. It is eerie, but it is true.

121

We may be just beginning to learn about the transmission of information between persons and between God and man. If God is personal in nature and we are to pray, "Our Father . . ." as Christ suggested (Matt. 6:9), then we should expect some sort of response in meaningful terms. It may be that our ability to tune in to God's frequency is blocked by our own self-centered absorption. Perhaps our sin is like "filling our receiving screens with snow." Yet occasionally people get very clear "pictures" of God's answer to a prayer in terms of a meaningful word or image. And whether the contact was actually with God or not, sometimes the depth of the experience carries with it the power to change the life of the person praying, and through him the lives of many others.

Several years ago a good friend named Alan told me about a startling encounter he had just been through. My friend is an intelligent professional man and in some ways a little cynical about things he hears. I certainly do not know if the experience had a transcendent reference, but my friend had been deeply moved by the account he related.

A Christian, an automobile salesman, who was a friend of Alan's, decided he was going to make hospital calls two days each week as a part of his response to Christ's admonition to visit the sick. During a routine telephone call to a man named Bennie Abernathy, with whom he had talked earlier about buying a new car, the salesman, Bert Johnson, reached his potential customer's wife. She said, "Mr. Johnson, I don't think my husband will be needing a new car. He is in the hospital and has incurable cancer. He will probably never get out."

Bert thought to himself, I'll go by to see him, just to say "Hello." When he got to the man's room in the hospital, he had a very superficial conversation. Bennie was nice enough, but Bert didn't know him very well and had no idea how he felt about death. Finally, just before leaving, Bert decided to get in at least a word about the real situation. He turned to the sick man, "Well, I hope the Lord gives you peace about all this," nodding toward his body.

When the man heard Bert, his face lighted with a wonderful smile. "Let me tell you something," he said. "All my life I have never really known what I felt about God. I have heard that a person must 'commit his life to Christ'; or 'be born again'—but I didn't really know how. Yesterday I was lying here very depressed because I did not know what to do to tie my life into God. In desperation I decided to pray. I simply asked God how I could come close to Him." The man's face was very sincere and intense as he remembered the experience. Now he looked into Bert's eyes with great clarity. "And do you know what happened as I prayed? I saw Jesus —here in this room, as real as you are. He was standing over there (he nodded toward the corner), and there were people coming to Him. As they got to where He was, each one would reach inside his own robe and lift out his heart . . . and hand it to Jesus. First there were grown men, all kinds, and then there were the children . . ." Bennie paused as he saw it all again in his mind against the wall in the corner of the room. Bert did not know how long they sat like that, but finally the man looked up calmly and said, "And I gave Him my heart too. He took it, put His other hand on my shoulder and smiled as He said, 'peace.' And then He was gone."

Bert could only nod his head slightly as if in agreement. "That's . . . wonderful," he said softly.

The man in the bed went on thoughtfully, "You know, Mr. Johnson, I realize this whole thing sounds absurd, but it's true. It's the truest thing that ever happened to me. And I am going to tell every person who comes in that door before I die."

And he did.

··+◆⦙◆+··

". . . All I can do is indicate indirectly certain events
in man's life, which can scarcely be described, which
experience spirit as meeting; and in the end, when indi-
rect indication is not enough, there is nothing for me but
to appeal, my reader, to the witness of your own mysteries—buried, perhaps, but still attainable."[37]

Martin Buber
I and Thou

"A miracle is 'not contrary to nature,' but contrary to
what we know as nature."[38]

Augustine
City of God

"In the dispute concerning the true God and the truth
of religion, there has never happened any miracle on the
side of error, and not of truth."[39]

Blaise Pascal
Pascal's Pensées

··+◆⦙◆+··

LORD, sometimes in my cynicism I feel as if prayer is auto-
suggestion and that we are playing games with ourselves
when we talk of communicating with You. And then I see the
miracles of modern science and realize that we are already
experiencing things which point beyond our intellectual horizons to a time when men in this life may be able to communicate mind to mind across thousands of miles. With regard to
You, we seem to see through a dim lens now; but I believe
with Paul that some day we may communicate face to face. I
believe, and I appreciate Your help with my unbelief.

··+◆⦙◆+··

"For our knowledge is imperfect and our prophecy is
imperfect; but when the perfect comes, the imperfect
will pass away. When I was a child, I spoke like a child,

I thought like a child, I reasoned like a child; when I became a man, I gave up childish ways. For now we see in a mirror dimly, but then face to face. Now I know in part; then I shall understand fully, even as I have been fully understood."

I Corinthians 13:9–12

A New Threshold

HURRAH! through several years of struggling to learn to live for God, I have been tiptoeing in a certain area. I have been very quiet about being a Christian when I am around atheistic philosophers and academic psychologists. I have let the humanism and scientism of some bright but ordinary minds intimidate me. But that is no longer the case. Recently I have realized that the assertion, "God *is*," is *at least* as philosophically sound as the belief that He is not. And after many years of checking this hypothesis as it is developed in the Christian gospel, I am persuaded that Christianity makes considerably more sense than atheism.

In struggling for my own handle by which to grasp the Christian faith with integrity, something profound has happened to me. As I was wrestling with the intellectual problems of believing, I was also learning to live a life in which I prayed, studied devotionally, and talked to other people about Christ. One day recently I was thinking about the gospel and logic when I realized that along the way somewhere I have become hopelessly in love with God. I have seen that experience comes alive and glows with light for me only as it revolves around His life and purposes as these are revealed in Christ and His people. I am suddenly and wonderfully not ashamed of my identification with the church.

How presumptuous and simple this must sound to anyone who has never ached and wept with frustration and disappointment over the church and the nature of its life, or lack of life, in the world. For years I have been free and proud to be a Christian in lay groups and at congregational meetings. But to be identified with the church in the academic world was a very difficult step. I have seen and been a part of so much of the sickness and soft thinking of the church that I have avoided this open identification for years—for fear I would lose forever the possibility of the respect of thinking men.

But now Christianity is coming into an historical perspective. I understand in a deeper way that the solutions to a divided world's problems politically and economically depend on a common acceptance of some Person or Purpose beyond any country's individual interests. I see God as the unifying hope for peace and international cooperation, really for the first time. I had read this notion years ago in Plato's Republic and heard it in sermons. But now I can grasp it at the depth of my being. Even as I write this, I am aware that such an abstract idea is politically naïve at this time. But I think that one day it will not be naïve at all.

I guess my own experience has taught me that the profound solution to the deepest human problems must wait until we have tried the more superficial answers involving our own clever manipulations. Then, when we see that outwitting our opponents does not win their love or loyalty and bring peace —then in our desperation, we may look into such "abstractions" as faith. And we may find that the truth of Christianity has in some strange way become personal, real, and very practical.

..+‡‡‡+..

". . . if many modern philosophers and men of science
could have had their way, they would have been dissuad-
ing Greeks, Jews, and Mohammedans from such useless
studies [as mathematics], from such pure abstractions
for which no foresight could divine the ghost of an
application. Luckily they could not get at their ances-
tors."[40]

Alfred North Whitehead
The Adventure of Ideas

WITH REGARD TO PROOF OF GOD:

"Perhaps the only thing that anyone can be absolutely
sure of is that he will never be able to prove it either way
—with objective, verifiable proof. We can know that in
the beginning there was God and not just some cosmic
upheaval that brought light out of darkness only when
we have experienced him doing the same thing in our
lives, our world—bringing light out of our darkness.

"To put it another way, unless there is some very real
sense in which the Spirit of God moves over the dark and
chaotic waters of this age, these deeps of yours and
mine; unless God speaks his light and life giving word
to me, then I do not really care much one way or the
other whether he set the whole show spinning x billion
of years ago."[41]

Frederick Buechner
The Magnificent Defeat

..+‡‡‡+..

LORD, thank You for the joy of discovery and for occasionally
allowing us to break through the fences of smaller mental
pastures into larger ones through faith. Help me to begin
looking at history, government, and economics as You see

them—rather than seeing only the personal issues of life. Help me never to be ashamed of You or Your message which is transforming my own experience of life. Give me a new dimension of freedom and courage to witness for You. This is a frightening threshold, Lord. The future is uncertain. Please give me Your hand.

·✦✦✢❙✣✦✦·

"For I am not ashamed of the gospel: it is the power of God for salvation to every one who has faith, to the Jew first and also to the Greek."

Romans 1:16

"For God has allowed us to know the secret of his plan, and it is this: he purposes in his sovereign will that all human history shall be consummated in Christ, that every thing that exists in Heaven or earth shall find its perfection and fulfillment in him."

Ephesians 1:9,10 (Phillips)

The Hinge Is Small

THE LONGER I am involved in the Christian life, the more clearly I see that the beginnings of significant life-long changes often hinge on seemingly insignificant discoveries and decisions in the intimate arena of personal relationships.

Some time ago about twelve of us got together to form a small group. We were trying to find out how we could learn to be God's people away from the church during the week. This was a new adventure which was exciting for most of the group. We decided that we would not tell anyone else what we were doing. The idea was to attempt various experiments in our lives during the week and then report to the group what happened to us.

Our plan was to begin in our families and work outward into the world. During the first week we were to look around, listen in our homes and see what *we* were doing to bug the people we live with, and then pray about our behavior to see if we could change it. Usually in prayer groups we had looked for those things other people were doing to bother us and then prayed for *them* to change. This is a very different approach.

The next week was an interesting one. One member of our group was a lovely, pleasingly plump, white-haired lady who was very attractive. At the first meeting I remember thinking that Lillian looked almost angelic . . . with a slight twinkle in her eye. She didn't seem to have any problems and prayed sweet, sincere prayers. Frankly, I wondered how she got in our group. Lillian had not said much so far, but she came into the next meeting like a rodeo rider out of chute four. She was so excited she was practically bubbling over. When I asked the group about the experiment, all Lillian could say was, "You all, it's the *shirts!*"

All I could think of to say was, "Would you like to talk about it?"

She went on, "I'm from the old South. And when I got married, my mother told me, 'Don't you ever iron any man's shirts. That's not wives' work.' So after the honeymoon twenty-five years ago, I told my husband I was not going to iron his shirts. He was a struggling student at that time, and we didn't have very much money, but he had to send his shirts out. After a few years, he developed a rash on his neck and had to wear shirts which required hand ironing. So for sixteen years Bill has been getting up on Saturday mornings and ironing his own shirts—right in front of me while I fixed breakfast. We were both Christians, but about that time we started going to different churches."

She stopped talking and put her fist against her mouth, and her bosom shook with an involuntary sob. In a moment she went on with tears in her eyes: "This week I discovered that all my guilt and self-hate as a woman, all of the wrangling and separation I've caused in our marriage, stems from the fact that I wouldn't iron Bill's shirts. I've prayed all week, and I don't know if I can do anything this late to change things for Bill . . . but I'd like for you to pray for me that I will." And we did.

Well, I don't know what Lillian did at home those next few

days, but the following week Bill showed up at the meeting, smiling from ear to ear. And they came to the group together regularly like two happy kids until Lillian died suddenly of a stroke a year later. But you know, that couple found each other, found a new kind of life together after twenty-five years.

What is that experience worth in terms of changing the world? I don't know, but watching it happen changed the rest of us in that group somehow. We began to see that the closed doors in our lives and relationships which we have been trying to batter down with argument and reason all these years—that those doors often swing open on small rusty hinges, on little things . . . like the shirts.

··◆◆❖❖❖◆··

"Indeed, this need of individuals to be right is so great that they are willing to sacrifice themselves, their relationships, and even love for it. This need to be right is also one which produces hostility and cruelty, and causes people to say things that shut them off from communication with both God and man."[42]

Ruel Howe
The Miracle of Dialogue

··◆◆❖❖❖◆··

LORD, help me to have the courage to look for the little inner walls and fortresses in my relationships, behind which I protect my pride. Forgive me for camouflaging these defenses and calling them "matters of principle" when so often they are only means to keep from having to admit that I have been wrong and wanted to be number one. I guess this is what has always made You so threatening to me. When You expose my self-justifying defenses, I either have to confess them or put You down . . . which is what I guess we tried to do on the Cross. And I still try to put You down when you get close to revealing the motives I have hidden. Help me, Lord, not to cling to my "rights" but to unclench my spiritual fist so that I can be free to follow You.

·⚬·◆◈◈◈◆·⚬·

"Let Christ Jesus be your example as to what your attitude should be. For he, who had always been God by nature, did not cling to his prerogatives as God's equal, but stripped himself of all privilege by consenting to be a slave . . . and . . . he humbled himself by living a life of utter obedience, even to the extent of dying . . ."

Philippians 2:5–8 (Phillips)

A Christian Father: The Artful Dodger

O NE OF THE most subtle problems I have found as a "committed and active" Christian is this: those of us who begin to minister to others sometimes start to take on a sort of Holy Immunity from some of the normal responsibilities of family life, because of our "high calling." For instance, any normal husband would catch hell if he were gone from home in the evenings half as much as the average minister is. Although it is true that I have often been as upset as my wife about having to be away from our family so much, it is also true that when the children were small, there was often a great relief in bypassing the thousands of details and questions with which our little girls plagued us in that rather frantic twilight period near the end of the day. And often when I was at home physically, I was absent emotionally.

Because of the lack of dependability of my presence with the girls when they were still quite young, Mary Allen was forced to assume the underlying responsibility for their growth and development. But the thing about this responsibility that seems to be particularly frustrating to wives is that it is only felt by the one who accepts it. So I did not even realize that there was such a burden, much less that I was not bearing my part of it. My ignorance of this problem led to no small amount of resentment in Mary Allen's life. She felt that to bring up my continual absence "for the Lord's work" would make her look like a lazy or nagging wife and a poor Christian. When she would bring it up, her tone was so loaded with resentment that I sort of felt she was those things.

But at a pastors and wives conference recently I counseled with a number of women, most of whom were married to prominent ministers. Several of them felt emotionally deserted with their children. And the husband, if confronted, had been irritated that the wife couldn't "do her part." Or he had retreated behind the ministerial shield with the guilt-provoking insinuation that however much he wishes it were different, "The Lord's work must come first." Some have even referred to the passage where Jesus' family came to get Him while he was speaking to a group, and He refused to come out (Mk. 3:31).

But as I began to see that these women were genuinely hurt, bewildered, and felt terribly alone with the emotional responsibility for their children, I started looking into it—especially since it seemed to be so common. That was when it occurred to me that *I* was doing the same thing to my own family.

Later, at home, I reread Mark 3:31 and discovered one thing immediately that would blast a legalist: When Jesus would not leave the group to whom He was ministering to go out to His family, He was talking about His *parental* family (mother and siblings). But He was not talking about leaving His wife and children in order to stay with the group to whom he was preaching.

I realize this may sound like scriptural nit-picking, but there is a great deal of difference in the responsibility for the

marital family one instigates and the parental family he is
supposed to leave. For in other places the Scriptures say that
a man is to give second place to his parental family and give
his *first* attention to the family represented by his marriage
(Gen. 2:24, Eph. 5:31). And of course the New Testament
Epistles are pretty clear about a Christian (particularly an
ordained minister) bearing his responsibilities to his wife
and children (Eph. 5:25, I Pet. 3:7, I Tim. 3:4, 12, 3:12 and
Tit. 1:6).

If this were true, I had a reorientation job on my hands
. . . with my own life. I began to realize that my unconscious
avoiding of a good bit of the constant nitty-gritty of family
living had made me hesitant to preach or teach about intimate
life in the home. And yet so much of the distress of new
Christians seemed to center in bruised family relations, but
how could I speak about problems I *still had?* So what I often
did was to avoid this issue and talk about "more important
matters" . . . like prayer or social involvement. And this way
I avoided facing the true nature of my holy immunity.

But as I continued to read about the life, death, and resurrection of Jesus Christ, I saw One who refused to witness or
preach from a favored position. Although He was probably
never married, He lived and witnessed out of an authentic life
in which He was as vulnerable as the people to whom He
ministered. I began to see that unless I can try to be a
genuine, participating father and husband, sharing the emotional responsibilities for my family's growth and happiness,
I have nothing to say about an authentic life in Christ to the
families around us.

How do I find a balance in all this? For I must be away
from home more than some men. And yet I must find a way to
include every member of my family in the shifting circle of
my inner emotional horizon. How do I build each one of them

into a calendar already filled with important and even necessary dates? I do not know how I can, but only that I must. (Tomorrow I will talk about some things I have tried.)

··+✦❖✦+··

"The 'great' commitment all too easily obscures the 'little' one. But without the humility and warmth which you have to develop in your relations to the few with whom you are personally involved, you will never be able to do anything for the many. Without them, you will live in a world of abstractions, where your solipsism, your greed for power, and your death wish lack the one opponent which is stronger than they—love."[43]

Dag Hammarskjold
Markings

··+✦❖✦+··

LORD, help me not to take myself and my work so seriously that I fail to be a husband and father to those special people You have given to me alone, to love and care for in Your name. If I fail with my mission as a witness to the community, You can raise others; but if I fail as a father to provide for the needs of those in my own home, there are no others to fill the void. This frightens me, Lord, because I don't know how to be a good husband and father, and I have let my own dreams and resentments keep me from facing my inadequacies. Help me to begin to learn how to be genuine and unselfishly loving in my own home.

··+✦❖✦+··

"If any one does not provide for his relatives, and especially for his own family, he has disowned the faith and is worse than an unbeliever."

I Timothy 5:8

An Injection for the Calendar

YESTERDAY, after I wrote about the problems of being a husband and father when one's calendar is loaded with trips and meetings, I jotted down some things which have been helpful to me in trying to move from the periphery toward the mainstream of our family's on-going life.

When I first started praying about trying to be a better father and husband, I made some disconcerting discoveries. In the first place I am controlled by habit to a larger extent than I realized. In certain ways I had put "other people" and "my ministry" (or business ventures) ahead of my family for so long, that I did not know how to begin changing without going overboard in the other direction.

These are some of the mechanical changes I made to get back into the bloodstream of our family's life: At the first of each year, I take my new appointment calendar and write on each family member's birthday, "Commitment to family." Then I do the same thing with our wedding anniversary, and I try to plan a vacation time with the family and put it on the calendar. For a while I added a couple of random two-day "commitments" so that Mary Allen and I could get away together. Later in the year, when some new project came up or someone called about a meeting which fell on one of the family's days, I said without any hesitation, "I'm sorry but I already have a commitment on that date."

I remember the first time an invitation to participate in a big meeting came on one of the children's birthdays. I was very interested in the meeting but said "no." The man, who was a friend, must have sensed my hesitation, because he asked, "Why can't you come? This is an important convention and your witness might reach a lot of people."

I was a little embarrassed to say that it was "my little girl's birthday," but I went on to tell him, "You can get half a dozen speakers in an hour, but I am the only daddy she's got."

He was quiet on the other end of the line for a few seconds, and I thought he had rejected me as a fool. Then he said quietly, "I wish I could do that." And I knew I had started in the right direction.

Before that time, I had been away on three family birthdays in a row. Now, I hardly ever miss a birthday unless something comes up that seems to warrant a very special exception, and we can all agree to slide the celebration to another date.

Another thing which has helped Mary Allen and me is to try to get a sitter and go out of town for a day or two by ourselves. We generally go to a nearby city to avoid the expenditure of time, money, and energy required for a long trip. We check in a hotel and relax. We may window-shop, read, see movies, eat quiet meals together, sleep late, and not even contact people we know well. These mini-vacations without the children help each of us know that we are being heard by the other and do something special for our relationship. I realize that many people cannot afford the money for this kind of "taking off." But we have gone when we could not afford it, and somehow the sacrifice has said to us that our relationship is very important. But if traveling is out, a little creative thought may help a couple to come up with another way to find time alone away from the children.

As to specific ways one relates to his wife and children at home, that which is natural for one man will not be for another. But the thing good fathers and husbands seem to have in common is the ability to make each member of the family feel important, and that old dad is "aware" of their needs and their accomplishments. The message I am trying to get across to my family is: "Although I am a busy person who will probably always be away from home some, each of you is very important to me. Among people, you are *first* in my life."

There have been times when this was impossible to say, because I was mad, or anxious, or because I was off trying to participate in the building of a new kingdom for God (or for me). But I try to come back again and again and build time for my family into the fabric of my life. I do this because I love them. And I have to resort to mechanical means because it is so easy for me to avoid the responsibility of thinking of anyone but me.

I may not make as many speeches, attend as many meetings, or write as many books for Christ. But I hope I will at least have lived for Him in my own home.

··+✛∰✛+··

"For the trouble is that we are self-centred, and no effort of the self can remove the self from the centre of its own endeavour; the very effort will plant it there the more fixedly than ever. The man of science is drawn out of himself as regards one whole range of his activity by the concentration of his attention on the object of his study in his search for truth; the artist, by a similar concentration in his search for beauty; the good man, or

public-spirited man, by a similar concentration in the
service of his cause. But none of these cover the whole of
life. Always there remains a self-centred area of life,
and sometimes by a natural process of compensation
those who are most selfless in the search for truth or
beauty, or in public service, are most selfish, fretful and
querulous at home."[44]

William Temple
Nature, Man and God

⋅⁺⊹⧟⊹⁺⋅

LORD, You know how many days I cannot turn loose and be a
good husband, how many times my mind is filled with visions
of my work or myself. Yet I want to be Your person in our
home. I love my family very much. But sometimes my behavior tells me I love what I am doing more. Help me to find a
balance, so I can be free in my work and yet enjoy being the
person my family needs.

⋅⁺⊹⧟⊹⁺⋅

"Enjoy life with the wife whom you love, all the days
of your vain life which he has given you under the sun,
because that is your portion in life and in your toil at
which you toil under the sun."

Ecclesiastes 9:9

An Earthen Vessel

THIS MORNING I am lonely. Mary Allen and the children are here, and we love each other very much. But I am facing some fears of failure which cannot be shared with them. I feel that my performance on a very important examination involving the future for all of us will not be adequate, and I'm anxious and afraid, like a small boy. Yet God seems very near. If I fail, He will be there, and I can pick up whatever pieces there are and do something else. And this gives me a deep underlying courage. But the conditioned franticness which makes my mind a beehive of fears is a carry-over from a lifetime of feeling that I must succeed to be acceptable.

This paradox is hard to understand—a sincere commitment to Christ combined with human insecurity in the face of failure. And many of the great Christian speakers and writers have left me alone in my predicament by neglecting to tell me of these paradoxes of the inner journey. As I have read devotional books and listened to the evangelists and teachers of the faith, I have tried to reconstruct from their words a picture of the inner way. But they have omitted so much of the sweat and gravel from their descriptions of the Christian life that I am left with visions of untroubled saints, walking through the quiet sterile corridors of their souls with unchanging attitudes of serenity and courage.

But I am finding that serenity and courage are very different in "appearance" from inside my own life. And as I counsel with other Christians, I realize that I am not alone in this. The record of Dietrich Bonhoeffer, as he wrote from the Nazi prison camp before his martyr's death, sounds stimulating and rather glorious at first glance. But as I read his letters* more closely, the actual daily experience *for Bonhoeffer* seems to have been very different. Much of it was made up of the buzzing whine of summer flies around his face, the maddening frustration and disappointment as his hopes for release were agonizingly prolonged or smashed, fear and doubts, and despair. All of these were things which often filled his mind as he lived out those days and nights of "marvelous Christian discipline and courage." Yet because of the paradoxical joy and hope he experienced, Bonhoeffer was able to go through that miserable imprisonment and make of it a great positive sign for all of Christendom. And this same paradox faces thousands of ordinary men and women who are trapped in jobs or marriages which seem impossible. But because they think that a "truly committed Christian" should *feel* victorious, they hide their painful loneliness and the guilt it brings.

This morning as I am confronted by the threat of changing to a new vocational direction in midstream of life with my bridges burned behind me, I *can* risk it because of my faith in Christ. But the fear of failure rides with me in the pit of my stomach as I go to the examination which determines the next chapter in our lives.

---

* Bonhoeffer, Dietrich, *Prisoner for God: Letters and Papers from Prison* (New York: The Macmillan Company, 1961).

If I pass the test and "succeed" in my new venture, some of my friends may say some day, "What courage, to have launched out in faith at your age!" And I wonder if I will remember the anxiety that makes my palms sweat as I write this. Or will I only smile, "give God the credit " humbly, and forget to tell how slender the thread of faith seems which I am following through the jungle of my fears right now?

·+·+‹‹||›+·+·

"I have repeatedly observed here how few there are who can make room for conflicting emotions at the same time. When the bombers come, they are all fear; when there is something good to eat, they are all greed . . . By contrast, Christianity plunges us into many different dimensions of life simultaneously."[45]

Dietrich Bonhoeffer
Prisoner for God

"It is rather in *overt* behavior that we must look for a measure of belief, and it is principally this that is inhibited in doubt or disbelief."[46]

D. E. Berlyne

·+·+‹‹||›+·+·

LORD, thank You that You give us the courage to go ahead and "risk it" occasionally in trying to follow You, forgiveness when we "chicken out" and cannot, and the clean slate of a new day after each of our failures and denials. In my attempts to witness to the hope and joy of Your presence in ordinary life, help me not to whitewash the frailty of the humanity into which it came to dwell as I try to trust You in everything. I am grateful that even You had some struggles in facing the challenges in Your life.

·+·+‹‹||›+·+·

"Anguish and dismay came over him, and . . . He went on a little, fell on his face in prayer, and said, 'My

Father, if it is possible, let this cup pass me by. Yet not as I will, but as thou wilt.' "

Jesus Christ
Matthew 26:38, 39 (NEB)

A New World in the Midst
of the Old One

A FUNNY THING happened this week. Our daughter Kristin, who is 15 years old, has been learning to drive. She is a very alert girl and is always aware of where we are and where we are going when we are out driving as a family. I am not. I often drive for blocks past a turn-off with my mind a thousand miles away. But Kristin is the one who often sits beside me and whispers, "This next block is our turn, Daddy." She knows our town with her eyes closed.

But this week when she got behind the wheel for the first time in traffic, it was as if we were in a new city: "Do I turn here, Daddy? . . . Is this the right street?"

I was amazed and thought at first that she was teasing me. But then I saw that she was not. A town that she had known like the back of her hand as a passenger became a strange and foreign place when she became responsible for the minute-by-minute decisions of driving. She had to look for a whole new set of objects and distances. She had to see cars backing out of driveways, puppy dogs and children starting for the street, vehicles at intersections, all kinds of street signs, in addition to everything behind her in the rear view mirror. With all of these new things on which to focus in the foreground of her

146

attention—which had heretofore been only a part of the background—she felt as if she were in a different world.

I started to fuss at her and tell her to "pay attention to what you are doing!" Then I realized that she was very serious and *was* paying attention. But she was experiencing a reorientation in the same situation because of trying to focus on different elements of her environment. So I said nothing and kept telling myself it was the end result of her training which was important.

As we drove along, I began to understand why it may be that newly committed Christians appear to be sort of "out of it." For a while, they seem to be like Kristin behind the wheel —in a kind of daze in which the world they have known appears to be totally different. Because of accepting the responsibility of a new relationship with God and focusing on loving Him and His people, they seem to be unaware of things and people to whom they once paid attention quite naturally. Many ministers or relatives are hurt and surprised when a church member gets "turned on" at some sort of lay renewal meeting and begins paying less attention to them because of his new Christian friends. They suspect that the new commitment was to a cult of some sort of self-centered pietists. The temptation is to be very judgmental of people experiencing this reorientation.

I do not know how one really ought to handle this situation. But by the end of the week (in our car) I noticed that Kristin knew where she was again. And now she can include both the old things she used to see . . . and the new things she needed to see to grow up and get on down the road.

·•◄❧►•·

"When we treat man as he is, we make him worse than he is. When we treat him as if he already were what he potentially could be, we make him what he should be."[47]

Goethe

"In training a horse, it is important not to break his spirit because it is his spirit, during and after the training period, which will determine his style and endurance. Does education, we may ask, allow for the expression of the wildness of vitality during the educational process, or does it repress vitality in the interest of form and conformity?"[48]

Reuel Howe
The Miracle of Dialogue

"A . . . peculiarity of the assurance state is the objective change which the world often appears to undergo. 'An appearance of newness beautifies every object.' "[49]

William James
Varieties of Religious Experience

·+◆≡▓▷+·

LORD, help us to be patient with new Christians who seem to have lost their perspective as they have entered a new relationship with You. If they become temporarily blinded to the ordinary responsibilities and the old friends around them, help us to provide an atmosphere in which this new relationship with You can be tested and translated into deeper relationships with people. Help us in the church to let new Christians enjoy the excitment of discovery without our hypercritical judgment—even though there may be some anxious moments about their soundness and responsibility.

·+◆≡▓▷+·

"And all were amazed and perplexed, saying to one another, 'What does this mean?' But others mocking said, 'They are filled with new wine.' "

Acts 2:12,13

"Therefore, if any one is in Christ, he is a new creation; the old has passed away, behold, the new has come."

II Corinthians 5:17

The Hardening of the Heart

THIS WEEK my prayers are filled with thoughts and plans of what I am going to do. I have been considering a new business venture. My mind is going over the proposal like a spider crawling around a baseball looking for a crack, a place to get inside the problems the business is supposed to solve. I am trying to determine whether a corporation or joint venture would be best for everyone involved. Since I was first attracted to the enterprise because it represented a possible solution to a problem in the church, I began with visions of how I would be doing God's work in the business. But more and more, the excitement centers around ways I could make a lot of money out of the deal.

I know that thinking about the profit potential is absolutely necessary before a business can be established. And I realize that a prayer time might be the best circumstance in which to consider a new business venture. But I have been disturbed by the course my own thoughts have taken about everything this week when I have prayed each morning. I have found myself becoming a calculating person, shrewdly assessing the day's activities and relationships in terms of financial criteria. Although it is very subtle, I have looked at the world as an orchard to be picked by me and for me and my family. The tricky part about what happened at this point is that other people did not seem to notice any change . . . at first. My outward responses were still basically positive toward people. But inside I developed a cool, detached feeling about them and found my thoughts were more manipulative than loving.

As the cycle continued its course, my family began to complain that I was grouchy, and they seemed to become a little "distant." I became terribly busy and started to feel somewhat isolated and empty. I finally woke up to the fact that my prayers were dry, that I was skipping them pretty regularly, and that I was beginning to be miserable inside. My heart felt cold toward God.

Today I have seen that this hardening process begins when I start getting grandiose visions of building great enterprises in which I am the center. And I recalled that this process has happened before. The road back to Christ is a hard one for me, because I cannot seem to realize the progressive way such thinking makes me preoccupied and causes me to stride roughshod over the feelings of those around me. I am like a tethered elephant stepping on his own brood.

But finally the "cold drafts" around the house and my own sense of busy isolation from God break through into my attention. And I realize that I have drifted away from being personal with Christ and with my family. At last, I have to confess that I have tried again to be "the King," to be God in my own little world . . . and that like a little boy with his candy, too much projected glory has made me spiritually sick at my stomach. I see that instead of following Christ, I have jogged ahead and tried to point out to Him the way we are to go.

I have subtly slipped the keys to my future out of His pocket and dropped them in mine. And I have to dig deeply and fork them over, telling Him that I really want to be His person and to participate in the doing of His will, instead of trying to be a Big Cheese in His world. Or if I cannot honestly tell Him that I *want* to do this, then I tell Him that I would like to want to.

When I can truly turn to Christ again in this way, a remarkable thing happens. I leave my time of prayer more open to those around me, less hard and more gentle. Somehow on such days I feel more at home in the world. And when I am dealing with people, I find myself seeking our mutual advantage in business instead of only mine. But I know I must stay close to Him with a daily surrender or I will be off again on my own. And it may take weeks for me to find out that I have picked the Lord's pocket and am galloping off over the cobblestones of my family's hearts with my future in my fist.

·•◄◄║►►•·

"Some there are that resign themselves, but with certain reservations, and put not their full trust in God; therefore they consider how best to provide for themselves. Some also at first offer all; but afterwards, having succumbed to temptation, they revert to their former state and make no progress in the path of virtue. These will obtain neither true freedom of heart nor the grace of My gracious friendship, unless with complete resignation, they offer themselves as a daily oblation unto Me. Without this surrender, there neither is, nor can be, any lasting and fruitful union with Me."[50]

Thomas à Kempis
The Imitation of Christ

". . . without thee all health is but the fuel, and all strength but the bellows of sin."[51]

John Donne
Private Devotions

·•◄◄║►►•·

THANK YOU, GOD, that You win our hearts not once, but again and again. I am grateful that You did not reject the disciples when they wanted to be the greatest. And thank You for the hope and confidence that You not only receive us prodigals back into your presence, but that You even put us to work in your vineyard again.

·⁖··⸎·

"No servant can be the slave of two masters; for either he will hate the first and love the second, or he will be devoted to the first and think nothing of the second. You cannot serve God and Money. . . ."

Jesus Christ
Luke 16:13 (NEB)

The Lack of Tangible
Results—a Problem

THIS IS ONE of those days when I am confused about Christianity. I believe; I am glad that I am a Christian— and yet nothing seems to happen of a lasting nature as a result of my witnessing for Christ. Knowing that this is a self-centered attitude doesn't seem to help much either.

In thinking about this problem of "results" just now, I remembered an early morning meeting yesterday with some men about whom I care a great deal. Charles Sumners, the minister of a large church in our city for more than thirty years, was speaking: "Sometimes I get discouraged. I can't see that my work with people is really changing anything. And as for my own belief in God, in a life after death, in the basic tenets of the faith—in the last analysis I am right where I was at the beginning of my ministry—I can only trust and hope that these things are true. Although I can see that realistically the church has grown and prospered in terms of members and material things, I cannot see that much has happened spiritually because of my ministry here."

No one said a word. We all love and respect this man a great deal, and he was baring his heart to us. As I sat in the silence, a picture passed through my mind. It was Sunday and Charles was standing in the pulpit. He was still quite weak after spending several days in the hospital and it was obvious to me that he was struggling with his sermon. But at the conclusion he told us that during his sickness he had seen once more the basic message of his ministry—that God loves us and has amazingly given us the gift of life in Christ. He became very enthusiastic and alive; it was as if he had just discovered this idea. I was afraid he might get too emotional, because of his weakened condition, and overtire himself. But at that point Charles stopped, looked at us with great calm, and concluded simply, "And I have found again in my own experience that I believe in Jesus Christ, and this belief is transforming my life."

Having finished his sermon, he sat down, probably discouraged again at our seeming lack of response. And yet my heart was singing. Somehow as he had said those words, filtered through a life which fairly radiated with courage and openness, I believed again too, and was excited with the renewed freshness of this discovery.

Then a young man in the prayer group yesterday morning responded to the minister's confession in an affirming way. And although the older man was grateful for the affirmation, it seemed to me he really could not accept it as true.

Since he was leaving town for a few days of rest, Charles excused himself from our group before the closing prayers. After he left, someone said thoughtfully, almost in amazement, "You know, he has *no idea* what the witness of his life has meant to those of us in his church." In the silence that followed a well-respected minister of another church said quietly . . . "In this whole *city*." In the closing prayers he poured out his gratitude for the strengthening influence of Charles Sumners in his own life and work. But of course

Charles did not hear the depth of gratitude the man expressed.

As the meeting broke up, it came to me: none of us can see with much accuracy the results of his own efforts, because so much of a Christian's influence has to do with the depth of his own personal inner life. To the Christian himself it seems like a battleground of losses and retreats, marred with old scars and shell holes. But from the *outside*, other people may see only the aura of love and concern which seem to surround those who commit themselves wholly to the finding and doing of God's will and the loving of His people.

I realize now that most of us will never be able to know accurately the long-term effects of anything we try to do. But it doesn't matter so much, because I can see that the kind of spiritual influence which appears to have deep roots and lasting affects is not usually projected consciously. Such influence seems to be a by-product of a style of living. People are evidently touched unconsciously through the Christian's eyes and hands as he tries to help them, and as he points beyond himself . . . to tell them about Christ and His healing love.

·⊷✦⊶·

"Even coherence with God's perfect will leaves reason in restless clash with the actual. Thus while faith can free reason from basic anxiety it can never rest it in any complacent solution."[52]

Nels Ferré
Faith and Reason

·⊷✦⊶·

DEAR GOD, I am very grateful that You left us the stories— like "the widow's mite"—about the importance to You of the efforts and gifts of ordinary people who have no great credentials in terms of fame and material statistics. Help me to remember that You do not judge as we do. And thank You that even as You give us peace, You give us a restlessness which moves us always beyond ourselves to seek and love other people. Thank You that You make me want to do great things for You, but thank You even more that Your love is not contingent on my getting them done.

⊷⊶

"Therefore, my beloved brethren, be steadfast, immovable, always abounding in the work of the Lord, knowing that in the Lord your labor is not in vain."

I Corinthians 15:58

Prayer: A Wisdom of Its Own

D O YOU BELIEVE that God is omniscient—that He knows all that we are thinking?" he asked me. I said that I did. The young man smiled with a little condescension as he sprang his logical trap, which was calculated to discredit the whole idea of prayer.

"Well, then," he continued, "if *He* already knows I have committed a particular sin and *I* already know it, doesn't it seem a little childish for me to tell *Him what He already knows?* Therefore, I see no logical reason for a Christian to confess anything to God."

I was with a sharp group of college students late one night at a leadership conference. The other Christian kids in the group seemed very interested in the boy's logic. I just felt tired. As I thought about his question, my mind went back to a marital counseling situation several years before and to something I had read fifteen years earlier by Randolph Crump Miller.*

"Let me set up a situation for you," I said. I asked the boy if he were married. He was. "Let's say you went home from this conference a day early," I continued, "and as you were

---

* Miller, Randolph Crump, *The Clue to Christian Education.*

going in your house you happened to notice the light on in the bedroom next door. Through the window you saw your wife in the act of committing adultery. Later she came home and said nothing about the affair with the neighbor. Now *you* already know she has sinned against your marriage, and *she* already knows it. But is there any real chance for a trusting, open relationship between you in the future unless she confesses to you *that which you both already know?*"

I watched the boy grasp the truth I had read years earlier and saw him shake his head at the apparent paradox of confession and restoration. I realized that he had been thinking about Christianity as another logical philosophical system, and that I think of it as a loving, family type relationship with God and with people. In our marriage Mary Allen and I have discovered that the dynamics of healthy intimate relations for us are ruled by a kind of personal wisdom and concern that transcend formal logic, and often seem to contradict it. Yet *within* such a good marriage, for instance, the rules and energy governing love, hate, failure, confession, forgiveness, and restoration have a profound and compelling kind of logic of their own, which those outside such a relationship can never grasp at a personal level.

As I drove home from the meeting that night I could remember a good many marriages, and even business partnerships, which had gone on the rocks—when "logic and justice" were substituted for the healing power of confession and forgiveness—even though all the parties already knew the *facts* about the broken relationship involved.

···✦···

"We are like earthworms, cabbages, and nebulae, objects of divine knowledge. But when we . . . assent with all our wills to be so known, then we treat ourselves, in relation to God, not as things but as persons. We have unveiled. Not that any veil could have baffled this sight. The change is in us. The passive changes to the active. Instead of merely being known, we show, we tell, we offer ourselves to view."[53]

C. S. Lewis
"Episcopalian"

"Through prayer, religion insists, things which cannot be realized in any other manner come about: energy which but for prayer would be bound is by prayer set free and operates in some part, be it objective or subjective, of the world of facts."[54]

William James
The Varieties of Religious Experience

LORD, thank You for the wisdom, the pattern, and the power of the continually reconciling relationship which you designed and revealed through the life, death, and resurrection of Jesus Christ. Help me to come to You and to tell You what I know about my sin; and then give me a new heart to love with today. When I am proud and want to bypass confession, then break my heart rather than let me only bow in Your direction and turn from You in my daily living. Stay with me, Lord, so I can stay with You.

"Create in me a clean heart, O God, and put a new and right spirit within me. Cast me not away from thy presence, and take not thy holy Spirit from me. . . . O Lord, open thou my lips, and my mouth shall show forth thy praise. For thou hast no delight in sacrifice; were I to give a burnt offering, thou wouldst not be pleased. The sacrifice acceptable to God is a broken spirit; a broken and contrite heart, O God, thou wilt not despise."

Psalm 51:10,11; 15–17

Resenting the People—A Minister's Trap . . . with Room for All

G OOD MORNING!" he said—too brightly, it seemed to me— "Did you get a good night's sleep?"

I just looked at him for a few seconds as he walked past me into my motel room. *He had to be kidding.* This man had brought me back to the motel after midnight from the meeting with college kids, *after* the reception, *after* the big meeting in the church's sanctuary . . . which had come *on the heels* of a small dinner party. I had arrived in town about five o'clock from an all day flight, following some similar marathon-type-church meetings the week before. Now at 6:30 the same morning he was picking me up to take me to an "informal breakfast" with about a hundred men to whom I was to speak. I was so tired that I felt a little sick at my stomach.

Actually, I liked the man who was standing there talking to me. He is a great guy and I think he is honest, courageous, and a deeply committed Christian minister. But something was definitely wrong between us. Then I recognized my feelings—resentment, raw resentment, and I had not even been able to admit it consciously. I was mad at myself, too, for letting him get me into all this. I recalled telling him over

160

the telephone that I was very tired and had three strenuous days of meetings immediately following my "stop off" with him. So he had originally planned a gathering for me to get acquainted with a few of the people who had been involved in small groups in his church. But the real purpose of my stopping, as I had understood it, was so that the minister and I could get acquainted.

The intimate dinner party was pleasant, but there was a large crowd at the evening meeting. Then after I spoke, there were thirty minutes of direct questions—followed by two later "unscheduled" meetings. To have refused to speak again would have seemed un-Christian, even though I was exhausted. I guess I had expected him to "protect me" or say "no" for me, but since he did not, I was resentful and was mad at myself too. Why was I angry, though? Everything had gone well, and I am committed to witnessing, to giving my life to Christ and His people. Yet I woke up resenting these fine church people, but I was not sure why. And as I stumbled to the next city to meet with a group of pastors, I was still wondering.

During one session of the pastors conference, I asked each of the participants to write on a slip of paper their most pressing problem as a person in being a minister. Going through the slips, I was surprised to find that one of their main problems was resentment of the people in their churches. Some felt that the members used them in thoughtless ways which they would not think of using a business associate. Some thought their people had tried to extract every ounce of work they could out of their pastor for the smallest possible salary. There were many other problems, but they added up to a feeling that they were not being treated as persons but were used as religious equipment.

And then it hit me. I was as much a professional religionist as these pastors, and I was getting a small taste of that which many ministers live with constantly. People—many of whom love him dearly—thoughtlessly make extra demands and set up situations in which the minister either has to participate or appear to be selfish and un-Christian. The pastor in this trap often goes along, wanting to be God's servant. But because he is exhausted and the expectations are unreasonable, he begins to feel depressed—beyond mere physical exhaustion. And he feels a strange tightening in his stomach when additional meetings are called or added "duties" are dumped into his lap. What I had seen in my own experience was that these symptoms resulted from a repressed resentment of the very people I had flown a thousand miles to love for God's sake. It was terrible but true.

I saw that my problem as a professional was that I was still too concerned with my own feelings of happiness and satisfaction. I realized that I lacked a sort of divine disinterest in how I am treated. But on the other hand, I saw that we laymen are often "people eaters" in that we devour the personal life and creative love of our pastors and spokesmen by the way we use them and fail to help them. And the strange thing is that we never know what we are doing to them on the inside. Some of them resent us for it, but because they have been trained that such resentment indicates self-centeredness in a Christian, they must repress it. So, many ministers become discouraged, sick (physically or emotionally), or leave the ministry. And they feel guilty and bitter. (Of course many others are evidently emotionally wired for ceaseless activity and find their fulfillment in going constantly.)

But I now realize that my problem, as a layman, is that I have not been aware of the suffering of ministers—which means I have not loved them enough to be sensitive to their needs.

In my own case, as a traveling speaker, I had to make a new beginning by confessing to God my resentment and frustration. I realized that a good bit of the problem that night was *mine* for not establishing concrete limits and staying roughly within them. This I can try to do in the future in order to have an intelligent ministry when I travel. And I am praying not to be so interested in *my* happiness and well-being.

When I got home from that trip, I examined our attitudes in our church and was appalled at what I saw. We seem to expect our ministers to run the church with fewer staff people than we would dream of allocating to an executive in a business venture of comparable size. We say we love our ministers and are very grateful for them. But somehow we do not really look at their needs the way we do those of "normal people."

It seems that I am so interested in my own hopes, dreams, and projects that I use other people to the limit—and yet I could not really recognize the extent of my own selfish tendency to use others . . . until it happened to me.

··◆◆۞◆۞◆◆··

"Tell me how much you know of the sufferings of your fellow men and I will tell you how much you have loved them."[55]

Helmut Thielicke
Our Heavenly Father

"The longer I live, the more I feel that true repose consists in 'renouncing' one's own self, by which I mean making up one's mind to admit that there is no importance whatever in being 'happy' or 'unhappy' in the usual meaning of the words. Personal success or personal satisfaction are not worth another thought if one does achieve them, or worth worrying about if they evade one or are slow in coming. All that is really worth while is action—faithful action, for the world, and in God. Before one can see that and live by it, there is a sort of threshold to cross, or a reversal to be made in what appears to be men's general habit of thought; but once that gesture has been made, what freedom is yours, freedom to work and to love! I have told you more than once that my life is now possessed by this 'disinterest' which I feel to be growing on me, while at the same time the deep-seated appetite, that calls me to all that is real at the heart of the real, continues to grow stronger."[56]

Pierre Teilhard de Chardin
Letters from a Traveller

LORD, forgive me. I was so intent on being treated well myself that I failed to see how thoughtless I often am in using the speakers I invite to visit our town. And I see in a hundred ways how I subtly use others to further my plans, and then send them on their way without realizing how they may feel. Thank You that it is not too late to look around and try to be more sensitive to the people with whom I work and live. Please give me the insight, the desire, and the strength to change.

FOR THE MINISTER IN ME:

"Do nothing from selfishness or conceit, but in humility count others better than yourselves. Let each of you look not only to his own interests, but also to the interests of others. Have this mind among yourselves, which you have in Christ Jesus, who, though he was in the form of God, did not count equality with God a thing to be grasped, but emptied himself, taking the form of a servant, being born in the likeness of men. And being found in human form he humbled himself and became obedient unto death, even death on a cross. Therefore God has highly exalted him and bestowed on him the name which is above every name, that at the name of Jesus every knee should bow, in heaven and on earth and under the earth, and every tongue confess that Jesus Christ is Lord, to the glory of God the Father."

Philippians 2:3–11

FOR THE LAYMAN IN ME:

"Bear one another's burdens, and so fulfill the law of Christ. . . . Let him who is taught the word share all good things with him who teaches. . . . So then, as we have opportunity, let us do good to all men, and especially to those who are of the household of faith."

Galatians 6:2,6,10

A View from Loner's Peak

YESTERDAY I talked to a very sharp and winsome man with a good sense of humor. Jack is a Christian minister, a district superintendent, whose position in his denomination makes him a pastor to fifty or sixty other ministers. He is handsome, intelligent, articulate, honest about himself, personally committed to Christ . . . and miserable.

As we talked, Jack told me that he felt basically lonely inside—even though he has a fine family and has done well in his vocation. He said that when he looked around at the other participants at ministers' meetings like the one we were attending, he felt as if many of his associates represented a kind of "in group" and had close personal friends with whom they came and roomed; but that he was not able to be as personal with other people as they seemed to be. In fact he felt that he had very few truly close personal friends at all, and that made him feel inadequate and lonely—even though he ministers to people constantly and is surrounded by "Christian friends."

As we talked, I thought about my own life inside and how often over the years I have felt like a "loner." I recall as a youngster moving to a new city and looking at groups of boys who seemed to be such close buddies and wishing I could be a real part of that which they seemed to be sharing. But then I became a part of such groups, and later fraternities, and was a leader in several. I was surprised to learn that, except in rare instances, "in group" members are not nearly as loving and vulnerable to each other about their real problems and aspirations as they appeared to be *from the outside*. I discovered the "façade of intimacy" which in-groups often wear. Some groups are together so much because their individual members' identity is wrapped up in their association with the group, rather than because of any deep personal relationships with its members. But this façade of intimacy is a well-guarded secret, a secret which makes probably millions of kids and adults feel inadequate if they do not have "lots of close friends who are 'in.' "

I am an outgoing person and have always moved toward people. Yet inwardly I am shy and reticent about imposing myself on those with whom I would most like to be friends. But as I have counseled with men and women who are successful materially and socially these past few years, I have found myself identifying with their feelings of inadequacy in this area of life so often that I began asking some of them how many really close personal friends they had. Many replied, "None." Some said, "One or two," but almost no one had more than five or six. After having moved more than a dozen times in twenty years of marriage, I realize that although there are many people we love, respond to, and enjoy being with on occasion, there are only a handful of people we feel are close friends.

All this made me wonder if perhaps many of us have been subtly conditioned to look for something which actually does not exist, except in a few cases—a place in life with a large number of intimate, totally open friends. In a busy active life one has the time and energy to be real friends with only a very few people on a continuing basis.

The lonely district superintendent with whom I was talking

yesterday seemed to be feeling guilty, rejected, and inadequate because he could not get a group of other district
superintendents to be totally open and loving friends. But as I
talked to some of the other men at the conference, I found that
most of them were guarded about being open concerning their
personal lives to anyone. Because of vocational vulnerability,
it may be even more difficult for ministers to be part of an
open sharing group, where each member reveals his true needs
and inadequacies, than it is for laymen. But the desire seems
to be intense to satisfy this restless longing to find like-minded
people with whom one can share the trials and joys of life. A
person who feels that he is in a subordinate role will not do
for this kind of friendship. So it would seem that ministers
are fortunate to have one close friend with whom they can be
totally honest.

I believe this restless yearning for completeness in relationships is universal. And although we try to fulfill it
through friends, mates, and children, it seems to me that this
restlessness can never truly be satisfied by people. I am becoming convinced that this deepest unrest is a longing for
complete union with God, which is planted in the fabric of
every man's life. Maybe Augustine was right when he said
that our hearts will always be restless until we find our ultimate rest in Him.

In my own life, I am more relaxed about my peers than I
ever have been. I feel closer to people with whom I work and
pray, since I do not expect them to fulfill an interprersonal
need which can be met only by God. And paradoxically, some
of us are becoming to each other the deeply sharing friends
for whom I have always longed.

"Great priests, saints like the Curé d'Ars, who have
seen into the hidden depths of thousands of souls, have,
nevertheless, remained men with few intimate friends.

No one is more lonely than a priest who has a vast ministry. He is isolated in a terrible desert by the secrets of his fellow men."[57]

Thomas Merton
No Man Is an Island

" 'A friend is one soul in two bodies.' Yet friendship implies few friends rather than many; he who has many friends has no 'friend'; and 'to be a friend to many people in the way of perfect friendship is impossible.' Fine friendship requires duration rather than fitful intensity . . ."[58]

Aristotle, *Ethics*

LORD, give me the grace not to try to force other people to give me the kind of unconditional acceptance and love that only You have to give. Help me not to reject them when they cannot be You. Thank You that in Christ *You* have offered to be the personal friend I have longed for—in whose unconditional love and acceptance I can sometimes find the courage to reach out to others. Help me to risk their rejection in order to introduce them to You and Your truth about living as a son in this complex world. Although I hate to admit it, I am glad that You went through the experience in Christ and with Paul of having to go it alone without friends during some trying times. It is comforting to know that you understand the feelings of a loner.

JESUS:
. . . "Then all the disciples forsook him and fled."
Matthew 26:56

"And about the ninth hour Jesus cried with a loud voice . . . 'My God, my God, why hast thou forsaken me?' "

Matthew 27:46

AND PAUL:

"Do your best to come to me soon. For Demas, in love with this present world, has deserted me and gone to Thessalonica; Crescens has gone to Galatia, Titus to Dalmatia. Luke alone is with me . . . At my first defense no one took my part; all deserted me . . ."

II Timothy 4:9–11, 16

Confessions of a False Prophet

For a long time after I became a Christian I did not speak about my faith publicly. But several years ago I began to travel and talk about the Christian life as it was unfolding in my own experience as a business man.

This was a good experience but a strange thing began to happen. As I traveled further and further from home, wrote a book, and spoke to larger groups, some people quit reacting to me as an ordinary layman who had made an exciting personal discovery. Certain individuals began to react to me as something other than a struggling Christian. A few started to treat me as some sort of "authority" or a "program personality" and to look after my physical comfort with great care and thoughtfulness when I was with them. I found this very pleasant. As a matter of fact, without ever realizing it, I began to expect this little bit of special care and status which was more and more being accorded me. And, although I have only seen it in retrospect, I noticed occasionally more than a tinge of resentment for those people who invited me to speak and did *not* make adequate arrangements for me while I was in their city. After all, I thought, I was often exhausted, since traveling and being with people constantly is very tiring for me.

But then it occurred to me what was happening. I was becoming the thing I have rebelled against all my life: a pampered professional religionist. With a kind of shocked thoughtfulness I could see what sometimes happens to ministers, bishops, and traveling evangelists. People seal them into a sort of emotionally padded traveling litter and pass them from one religious group or situation to another. They do not treat such visiting pros the same way they treat other men at all. The difference is very subtle and built into our social response system; and most people do not seem to realize that they are treating "religious speakers" with such deference.

But after a while the effect can be very corroding to the speaker's integrity. At one level or another he begins in self-defense to fit the role expected of him and become a religious authority, instead of a person who wants to live out his life trying to find and do God's will. And if a speaker surrenders to this temptation to be "outstanding," there is a fantastic danger, it appears to me, of becoming an "approval-holic": hooked on constant favorable attention and approval instead of alcohol. When I move in this direction it affects subtly but deeply the *content* of my speaking as well as its freshness. I unconsciously tone down the unpleasant aspects of that which I am saying and accentuate those things which affirm the group's existing beliefs and prejudices. And before long I will have justified the whole procedure by telling myself that I should be gentle and go slowly with people.

Several ministers over the years have told me in one way or another, "Keith, I really believe in a committed life. But my people are not ready for that kind of commitment yet, or that kind of confrontation." So they admit they preach something less than the best they know and have experienced, because they are afraid people "are not ready" for the best. But when this happened to me recently and I said these same words to myself, I discovered that I meant by them that it was *I* who was not ready to risk a certain group's rejection of *me* if I said things which were too threatening to their beliefs . . . and thus to the status quo. So for that night I became what the Scriptures call a "false prophet," more interested in material approval than in speaking any creative, freeing truth God had given me.

But the tragedy is that with all of my recognition of and rebellion against these things, I find myself very subtly doing them. At the time my reasons seem so sound, and sometimes I realize they are sound. And often I catch myself and do speak the truth as I see it. But here in this time of prayer I know that I am still so often full of myself and concerned about what people think of me. And I know that I am deeply a part of the problem for which Christ died.

·⬦⬦⬦·

A PROPHET:

"He broke fresh ground—because, and only because, he had the courage to go ahead without asking whether others were following or even understood. He had no need for the divided responsibility in which others seek to be safe from ridicule, because he had been granted a faith which required no confirmation—a contact with reality, light and intense like the touch of a loved hand; a union in self-surrender without self-destruction, where his heart was lucid and his mind loving . . ."

CHARACTER OR TOLERANCE?

"All too easily we confuse a fear of standing up for our beliefs, a tendency to be more influenced by the convictions of others than by our own, or simply a lack of conviction—with the need that the strong and mature feel to give full weight to the arguments of the other side. A game of hide-and-seek: when the devil wishes to play on our lack of character, he calls it tolerance, and when he wants to stifle our first attempts to learn tolerance, he calls it lack of character."[59]

Dag Hammarskjold
Markings

··+✛+··

LORD, help me to begin again with Your strength and Spirit, and to be one of the free children of Your family. Help me to speak to please You and not important or brilliant people. Allow me to transmit something of the love and creative courage You showed us in Christ. Forgive me when I am afraid to chance rejection or failure. But thank You for the times I am willing to risk being vulnerable in love. May their number increase.

··+✛+··

". . . though we had already suffered and been shamefully treated at Philippi, as you know, we had courage in our God to declare to you the gospel of God in the face of great opposition. For our appeal does not spring from error or uncleanness, nor is it made with guile; but just as we have been approved by God to be entrusted with the gospel, so we speak, not to please men, but to please God who tests our hearts."

I Thessalonians 2:2–4

The Gamble of Faith

YESTERDAY MORNING I woke up restless and vaguely afraid . . . of what I wasn't sure. Then I remembered: in the mail the day before I had received a letter from a dear friend. He had just been advised by his doctor that he had between two weeks and three months to live because of a malignancy which had reached his liver. I was deeply shaken and grieved. The vague anxieties I had felt earlier blossomed into concrete fears, and I began to imagine all kinds of bad things happening.

Over a year ago I decided to devote my time to writing professionally, without the support of a regular job. But I have been doing so much public speaking and traveling that I worry about not getting any writing done and not being able to make a living for my family. As the specters danced out of the shadowy corners into my conscious mind, I imagined Mary Allen's death and my great loneliness at her dying . . . the children had grown up and left home . . . I was a lonely old man. Then, like a jack-in-the-box, out jumped the specter of my own death, and I was afraid. I did not know in that instant whether I believed in Christ or even in God the Father. I experienced the great emptiness of death, was horrified . . . and desperately wanted proof and certainty.

175

But as I saw these things and faced the panic they brought, I also grasped again with pristine clarity the deep human meaning of the gospel of Jesus Christ for me. "Let not your hearts be troubled . . ." (Jn. 14:1), "I go to prepare a place for you . . ." (Jn. 14:3), "be of good cheer, I have overcome the world" (Jn. 16:33). I saw that I could not capture faith once and for all time and put it in a box for safekeeping. In the face of death and possible failure in my own life or in the lives of those I love, I could not even *know* for sure that "God is."

"What am I going to do?" I thought, trying not to give in to the wave of desperation I felt was about to break over me. I had lived with faith for years, and it seemed to be crumbling all around me. Then I knew. All I could do, to come to terms with my own death, was to bet my life that Jesus Christ "is for real," and give Him my whole future.

It became evident to me again that this Christian Way is not often entered through the lofty door of philosophical reasoning, but through a wager, a bet with fantastic stakes.* Because of those things I have seen and heard in my own experience and in the lives of many others across the years, I have bet my life that God *is*, and that He is the kind of love which walked around in the life and actions of Jesus Christ. I have wagered that He even loves me and wants me to be related as a child to Him. And when out of great need, I have made this bet, I have stepped into a new dimension of life— life in which there is hope in history because God is at the end of the road for me and for all of us.

---

* This notion of a wager may seem strange or not respectable. I got the idea from Blaise Pascal the 17th-century mathematical genius who had a profound Christian conversion. As he pointed out, one makes the wager that God is or is not either consciously or implicitly by his behavior. I am just suggesting that it has been helpful to me to make it explicit. See Pascal's *Pensées*.

Now, although I still cannot *know* that God is real, I somehow *do* know. Even though I cannot prove it to you or even make the bet for you, I can say this: for me, these seem to be the only two alternatives—to live a phony life of frantic hiding from myself and of psychological repression of thoughts about death and meaning. Or to face death and life and make this strange gamble of faith which turns me outward toward other people and makes me want to be a loving person. I can see no other way for me than following Christ.

··+·❀❀·+··

"We all want to be certain, we all want proof, but the kind of proof that we tend to want—scientifically or philosophically demonstrable proof that would silence all doubts once and for all—would not in the long run, I think answer the fearful depths of our need at all. For what we need to know, of course, is not just that God exists, not just that beyond the steely brightness of the stars there is a cosmic intelligence of some kind that keeps the whole show going, but that there is a God right here in the thick of our day-by-day lives who may not be writing messages about Himself in the stars but who in one way or another is trying to get messages through our blindness as we move around down here knee-deep in the fragrant muck and misery and marvel of the world. It is not objective proof of God's existence that we want but, whether we use religious language for it or not, the experience of God's presence. That is the miracle that we are really after. And that is also, I think, the miracle that we really get."[60]

Frederick Buechner
The Magnificent Defeat

··+·❀❀·+··

LORD, I do love You. And I am very grateful that this relationship with You has been so often one of hope and a sense of expansion into a larger and more interesting journey. But occasionally there are these times of dread and doubt which bring me to my knees in awe. I see again that faith is a gift of grace, and that all the figuring and reasoning in the world cannot transpose me across the void between us and You. Thank You that in Christ You have provided the leap of faith, the fantastic wager of life.

"I sought the Lord, and he answered me, and delivered me from all my fears."

Psalm 34:4

Renewal in the Church—But
Who Cares Enough?

B<small>UT THE PEOPLE</small> don't really care that much," the bright, young minister was saying in a thoughtful but discouraged tone. We had just finished a series of meetings in his church, and he had gotten a large group of apparently interested men and women out for every session. I had just said that it was obvious he had done some work among these people—especially since so many ministers had told me that they could not motivate their congregations to do anything besides attend Sunday services.

But this very perceptive young man saw beyond the meetings into the people's lives. He knew that his affluent congregation was really living for money, social status, and power. And he saw that all this "church business" was only a small part of a more important social life for most of his members. "How can people like this ever be vehicles for new life in the Church?" he asked, shaking his head in answer to his own question. He smiled philosophically as he shook my hand at gate No. 4, and I got on the plane for New York and Boston.

I tried to settle down in a coach window seat, hoping to relax a few minutes before the next churchful of strangers.

Thinking about the congregation I had just left and its young
pastor's remarks, I began to feel that he was right: people
whose imaginations are captured by the world—even the
good things in it including church business—are not going to
be motivated strongly enough to take the risks and discipline
necessary for genuine newness to come in the Church. But
what kind of people will be motivated to stick with it?

I did not want to think about it any more, so I closed my
eyes and prayed: "God, I'm tired—tired of thinking about
these same problems, tired of traveling, tired of being a misfit
in a generation going in a different direction from the one I've
chosen." As I continued talking to God, I found myself saying, "But I wouldn't trade what I've found in this relationship
with You for all the geographical settledness in the world. I
guess I just remember too well the fear and blankness of
living without You. Somehow Your presence and acceptance
here and now make this perpetual wandering seem almost
like a home."

Opening my eyes, I smiled at the hostess, accepting a cup
of coffee. I had been in a semi-conscious state, pretty oblivious of the plane. But I waked up with a deep conviction
about new life in the institutional church: I was convinced
that "Christian renewal" will be accomplished—where it takes
place with any lasting depth—through the lives of a group of
desperate people who are personally finding irreplaceable
hope and meaning in living for Christ and His purposes
among men. Because, as the young minister had said so
perceptively, the ordinary busy churchmen "really don't care
that much."

·+◄⊰⊱►+·

[Christian meets Worldly Wisdom who tries to dissuade
him from going on the Christian pilgrimage] "I am
older than thou; thou art like to meet with, in the way

which thou goest, wearisomeness, painfulness, hunger, perils, nakedness, sword, lions, dragons, darkness, and, in a word, death, and what not . . . And why should a man so carelessly cast away himself by giving heed to a stranger [and going on]?

"Christian: Why, sir, this burden upon my back is more terrible to me than are all these things which you have mentioned: nay, me thinks I care not what I meet with in the way, if so be I can also meet with deliverance from my burden."[61]

John Bunyan
Pilgrim's Progress

"For the son of God did not come from above to add an external form of worship to the several ways of life that are in the world, and so leave people to live as they did before. But he came down from heaven altogether divine and heavenly in his own nature to call mankind to a divine and heavenly life; to the highest change of their own nature; to be born again of the Holy Spirit; to walk in the wisdom and light of God; to be like him to the utmost of their power; to renounce all the most plausible ways of the world; and to live in such wisdom, purity, and holiness as might fit them to be glorious in the enjoyment of God to all eternity."[62]

William Law
*A Serious Call to a Devout and
Holy Life*

LORD, thank You that we are only asked to penetrate the world and not engulf it. I am grateful You intimated that a little salt—a few committed people—can do the job of changing the taste of the whole banquet of life to which You have invited all men. Help me to seek out those other men and women in Your Church whose needs are such that they cannot live without You, those other people who clearly know they need a Physician. Bring us to life, Lord, as Your people. Help us to wake up; and fill us with the power and the Spirit to be Your gentle giants in the world, in which we live as Your hesitant children.

·•❊❊❊•·

"Besides this you know what hour it is, how it is full time now for you to wake from sleep. For salvation is nearer to us now than when we first believed; the night is far gone, the day is at hand. Let us then cast off the works of darkness and put on the armor of light."

Romans 13:11,12

I Needed My Past

SOMETIMES WHEN ONE of our children feels rejected by a group, or thinks she is unattractive and unacceptable, my stomach tightens and I ache for them. I want to run and hold my little girl and protect her from the pain and rejection of the world. But at such moments I am never sure exactly how to pray. Because every time the situation comes up, I remember Alice's face one night many years ago.

We were in a small group of adults who were struggling together to learn how to pray and to live as Christians. We were getting acquainted by going around the room, each telling the others some things about his childhood. One older lady had had a good many disappointments and seemed bitter about her past. Then it was Alice's turn. She spoke to us hesitantly.

"When I was a tiny little girl, I was put in an orphanage. I was not pretty at all, and no one wanted me. But I can recall longing to be adopted and loved by a family as far back as I can remember. I thought about it day and night. But everything I did seemed to go wrong. I tried too hard to please everybody who came to look me over, and all I did was drive people away. Then one day the head of the orphanage told me a family was going to come and take me home with them. I

183

was so excited, I jumped up and down and cried. The matron reminded me that I was on trial and that it might not be a permanent arrangement. But I just knew it would be. So I went with this family and started to school in their town—a very happy little girl. And life began to open for me, just a little.

"But one day, a few months later, I skipped home from school and ran in the front door of the big old house we lived in. No one was at home, but there in the middle of the front hall was my battered old suitcase with my little coat thrown over it. As I stood there and looked at that suitcase, it slowly dawned on me what it meant . . . they didn't want me. And I hadn't even suspected."

Alice stopped speaking a moment, but we didn't notice. We were each standing in that front hall with the high ceiling, looking at the battered suitcase and trying not to cry. Then Alice cleared her throat and said almost matter-of-factly, "That happened to me seven times before I was thirteen years old."

I looked at this tall, forty-year-old, gray-haired woman sitting across the room and wept. I had just met Alice, but I found myself loving her and feeling a great compassion for her. She looked up, surprised and touched at what had happened to us as we had responded to her story. But she held up her hand and shook her head slightly, in a gesture to stop us from feeling sorry for her. "Don't," she said with a genuinely happy smile, "I *needed* my past. You see—it brought me to God."

·✦·

"Can this be true? Is there any greater wretchedness than to taste the dregs of our own insufficiency and misery and hopelessness, and to know that we are certainly worth nothing at all? Yet it is blessed to be reduced to these depths if, in them, we can find God. Until we have reached the bottom of the abyss, there is still something for us to choose between all and nothing. There is still something in between. We can still evade the decision. When we are reduced to our last extreme, there is no further evasion. The choice is a terrible one. It is made in the heart of darkness, but with an intuition that is unbearable by its angelic clarity: when we who have been destroyed and seem to be in hell miraculously choose God!"[63]

Thomas Merton
No Man Is an Island

DEAR LORD, help me to remember that You did not promise to take us out of the problems of the world, but that You did promise to be with us as we face them. Give me the faith and the courage to let my children live and take their knocks without panicking. And when they fail, help me to stand by them as they try to pick up the pieces and move into the future. Help me to give them support but not to over-protect them from the difficulties of growing up, since I remember that I, like Alice, needed the problems of my past to bring me to You.

"Indeed I count everything as loss because of the surpassing worth of knowing Christ Jesus my Lord. For his sake I have suffered the loss of all things, and count them as refuse, in order that I may gain Christ and be found in him, not having a righteousness of my own, based on law, but that which is through faith in Christ, the righteousness from God that depends on faith; that I may know him and the power of his resurrection, and may share his sufferings, becoming like him in his death, that if possible I may attain the resurrection from the dead."

Philippians 3:8–11

Notes

1. Dietrich Bonhoeffer, *Prisoner for God* (New York: The Macmillan Company, 1961), p. 52.
2. Louis Fischer, *Gandhi, His Life and Message for the World* (New York: Mentor Books, 1960), p. 33f.
3. Viktor E. Frankl, *Man's Search for Meaning* (New York: Washington Square Press, Inc., 1964), p. 158.
4. William James, *The Varieties of Religious Experience* (New York: The Modern Library, 1929), pp. 452, 453.
5. Martin Luther, *Luther's Works* (Philadelphia: Muhlenburg Press, 1959), Vol. 36, p. 86.
6. Paul Tournier, *The Meaning of Persons* (New York: Harper and Row, Publishers, 1957), pp. 36, 37.
7. J. S. Whale, *Christian Doctrine* (Cambridge: The University Press, 1956), pp. 145, 146.
8. C. G. Jung, *The Collected Works* (New York: Pantheon Press, 1960), Vol. 8, see pp. 45–61.
9. Martin Luther, *Luther's Works* (St. Louis: Concordia Publishing House, 1959), Vol. 23, p. 73.
10. Thomas à Kempis, *The Imitation of Christ* (London: Collins, 1957), p. 90.
11. Paul Tournier, *Guilt and Grace* (New York: Harper and Row, Publishers, 1962), pp. 85, 86.
12. Paul Tournier, *The Adventure of Living* (New York: Harper and Row, Publishers, 1963), p. 116.
13. Fr. William McNamara, *The Art of Being Human* (Milwaukee: The Bruce Publishing Company, 1962), p. 69.
14. Rollo May, *The Art of Counseling* (New York: Abingdon-Cokesbury Press, 1939).
15. Will Durant, *The Story of Philosophy* (New York: Garden City Publishing Company, Inc., 1943), p. 52.
16. Alfred Adler, *Psychologies of 1930,* ed. Carl Murchison (Worcester, Mass.: Clark University Press, 1930), see chapter 21, "Individual Psychology."
17. William Temple, *Nature, Man and God* (New York: The Macmillan Company, 1956), p. 233.

18. Augustine, Bishop of Hippo, *The Confessions of St. Augustine* (New York: E. P. Dutton and Company, Inc., 1951), p. 187.

19. Lorenzo Scupoli, *Unseen Warfare* (London: Faber and Faber Limited, 1952), pp. 31, 32.

20. Paul Tillich, *The Shaking of the Foundations* (London: SCM Press, 1949).

21. Whale, *op. cit.*

22. Thomas Merton, *No Man Is an Island* (New York: Harcourt, Brace and World, Inc., 1955), p. 5.

23. Father Andrew, *The Life and Letters of Father Andrew*, ed. Kathleen E. Burne (London: A. R. Mowbray and Co., 1961), p. 166.

24. John Knox, *Life in Jesus Christ* (New York: Seabury Press, 1966), pp. 125, 126.

25. William Temple, *Readings in St. John's Gospel* (London: The Macmillan Company, Ltd., 1963), p. 24.

26. Sigmund Freud, *A General Introduction to Psychoanalysis* (New York: Washington Square Press, Inc.), p. 22.

27. William Barclay, *Turning to God* (London: Epworth Press, 1963), pp. 40, 41.

28. Frederick Buechner, *The Magnificent Defeat* (New York: The Seabury Press, 1966), p. 47.

29. D. Elton Trueblood, *A Place to Stand* (New York: Harper and Row, Publishers, 1969), p. 43.

30. Scupoli, *op. cit.*, pp. 96, 97.

31. Fischer, *op. cit.*, p. 33.

32. Scupoli, *op. cit.*

33. Thomas à Kempis, *op. cit.*, pp. 148, 149.

34. Frederick B. Speakman, *The Salty Tang* (Westwood, New Jersey: Fleming H. Revell Company, 1954), p. 97.

35. Paul Tournier, *The Meaning of Persons* (New York: Harper and Row, Publishers, 1957), p. 22.

36. Scupoli, *op. cit.*, p. 175.

37. Martin Buber, *I and Thou* (New York: Charles Scribner's Sons, 1958), p. 127.

38. Aurelius Augustinus, *The City of God* (New York: Modern Library, 1950), Book xxi, chapter vii, p. 776.

39. Blaise Pascal, *Pascal's Pensées* (New York: E. P. Dutton and Co., Inc., 1958).

40. Alfred North Whitehead, *Adventure of Ideas* (New York: Mentor Books, 1960), p. 160.

41. Buechner, *op. cit.*, p. 23.

42. Reuel Howe, *The Miracle of Dialogue* (Greenwich, Conn.: The Seabury Press, 1963), p. 93.

43. Dag Hammarskjold, *Markings* (New York: Alfred A. Knopf, 1966), p. 133.

44. Temple, *op. cit.*, p. 243.

45. Bonhoeffer, *op. cit.*, pp. 141, 142.

46. C. W. Morris, *Signs, Language and Behavior* (New York: Prentice Hall, 1946).

47. Morris E. Eson, *Psychological Foundations of Education* (New York: Holt, Rinehart and Winston, Inc., 1965), p. 39.

48. Howe, *op. cit.*, p. 124.

49. James, *op. cit.*, p. 243.

50. Thomas à Kempis, *op. cit.*, p. 181.

51. John Donne, *Private Devotions* (Ann Arbor, Michigan: The University of Michigan Press, 1959), p. 27.

52. Nels F. S. Ferré, *Faith and Reason* (New York: Harper and Row, Publishers, 1946), pp. 234, 235, footnote.

53. C. S. Lewis, "The Episcopalian," February 1964, p. 23.

54. James, *op. cit.*, p. 456.

55. Helmut Thielicke, *Our Heavenly Father* (New York: Harper and Row, Publishers, 1960), p. 93.

56. Pierre Teilhard De Chardin, *Letters from a Traveller* (New York: Harper and Row, Publishers, 1962), p. 160.

57. Merton, *op. cit.*, p. 12.

58. Durant, *op. cit.*, p. 62.

59. Hammarskjold, *op. cit.*, p. 110.

60. Buechner, *op. cit.*

61. John Bunyan, *Pilgrim's Progress* (New York: The Mershon Company), p. 14, 15.

62. William Law, *A Serious Call to a Devout and Holy Life* (Philadelphia: The Westminster Press, 1955), p. 69.

63. Merton, *op. cit.*, p. 208.